A Language Testing Handbook

by Andrew Harrison

Essential Language Teaching Series

General Editor: Roger H Flavell

MACMILLAN
PUBLISHERS

First published 1983
Reprinted 1986

Published by *Macmillan Publishers Ltd*
London and Basingstoke
*Associated companies and representatives in Accra,
Auckland, Delhi, Dublin, Gaborone, Hamburg, Harare,
Hong Kong, Kuala Lumpur, Lagos, Manzini, Melbourne,
Mexico City, Nairobi, New York, Singapore, Tokyo.*

ISBN 0–333–27174–2

Printed in Hong Kong

Contents

List of test types and applications

code letter	test type	placement	diagnostic	achievement	proficiency
A	scripted speech + true/false items	1	3	3	3
B	narrative text + true/false items	1	3	3	3
C	structured writing	1	2	2	2
D	cloze	1	x	2	2
E	dictation	1	2	2	2
F	conversation	1	x	2	2
G	scripted speech + multiple-choice pictures	x	1	3	x
H	scripted speech + completion items	x	1	3	x
J	completion + write	x	1	2	x
K	completion + multiple-choice fillers	x	1	3	x
L	transposition	x	1	2	x
M	unscripted speech + multiple-choice items	2	3	1	2
N	unscripted speech + visuals	2	3	1	1
O	text and argument + multiple-choice items	2	3	1	2
P	letter	2	3	1	2
Q	reorientation	x	2	1	x
R	speak to pictures	2	2	1	3
S	talk on topic	2	x	1	1
T	transfer	3	3	2	1
U	follow instructions	2	2	2	1
V	give advice	x	2	3	1
W	appropriate response	x	3	2	1
X	sequence	x	3	3	1
Y	role play	x	2	2	1
Z	problem solving	x	x	2	1

Note: The numbers indicate how useful each type of test is likely to be for the four purposes, placement, diagnostic, achievement and proficiency, ranging from 1 (most useful) to 3 (useful only in some circumstances); x means not suitable for this purpose.

Note

*An asterisk in the text means that the word or phrase alongside it
is explained in the Glossary beginning on page 140.*

Introduction

A common view of testing is that it is quite separate from teaching and learning, both theoretically and in practice. According to this view, a test is a necessary but unpleasant imposition from outside the classroom: it helps to set standards but uses up valuable class time. Underlying this book is the belief that, far from being divorced from each other, testing and teaching are closely interrelated. A test is seen as a natural extension of classroom work, providing teacher and student with useful information that can serve each as a basis for improvement.

The usefulness of the information derived from a test will depend upon the amount of care that is taken in its preparation. There seems to be a widespread belief that good tests are produced only by experts familiar with technical concepts and statistics. However, once it is accepted that testing is an integral part of teaching, it follows that the person best prepared to set the test is the teacher. When testing procedures are related more to teaching and learning than to theories of psychometrics (measurement of the mind) and statistical probabilities, then the experienced teacher is already halfway to being a test setter. What he still has to learn is how the principles and techniques of testing differ from those of teaching, and how to apply them.

This book falls into three parts. The first part (Chapters 1–3) is important for those who have no previous experience of testing, because it explains the concepts and principles on which the rest of the book is based. More experienced testers, however, should also find it useful as an introduction to the second part (Chapters

4–7), which offers a wide range of ideas for different types of test. The intention here is not to give a complete survey of all varieties of language test: this ground is already well covered by other books (see bibliography, page 136). The aim is to provide guidelines for setting several kinds of test which will be practical in use and give helpful information to both teachers and students about their successes and failings. The examples which illustrate the discussion are mainly invented for the purpose and are not meant to be used directly in the classroom. The reason for this is that a good test, like a good suit, should be made for the individual customer ('made to measure' is perhaps too ambiguous a phrase in the present context). The teacher must choose among the tests and techniques available, and adapt them to fit his particular situation. Finally, Chapter 8 takes up matters related to marking, while Chapter 9 gives a brief account of procedures which will help teachers to find out how well their tests have worked and to interpret students' scores.

It will be clear by now that the book is concerned with tests set by teachers for their own students, and not with external examinations such as those set by the Cambridge Syndicate or the Royal Society of Arts. The starting point for the tests in this book is always teaching and learning, with the assumption that the teacher's aim in the long run is to equip his students not with a general knowledge of grammar and vocabulary but with the particular language skills that they will need as, for example, a tourist or postgraduate. This means that the principles of the communicative approach to language teaching are never far from the surface, although the word 'communicative' itself is little used in the text.

A consequence of this approach is that each test is designed as far as possible from the point of view of the student taking it. Once the various skills needed by the student to do the test are properly set out, it becomes clear that test descriptions like 'reading comprehension' and 'oral' are not sufficient to indicate what the test is assessing. The titles given to the tests described in Chapters 4–7 may seem unconventional, but they are an attempt to show that a test does not assess skills in isolation from each other, or even in pairs, but in complex interactions which the student must cope with in order to complete the task set by the test.

1   Types of test

One of the arguments for an approach to testing through teaching and learning is that the teacher is in the best position to know which tests are appropriate for his class. The appropriateness of a test is largely determined by purpose: why is a test needed at a particular stage in the students' learning and what use will be made of the results? The four types of test described in this book are: placement, diagnostic, achievement and proficiency, though the categories of test and the names given to them vary considerably according to the preferences of different writers. Figure 1 shows the general content, the purpose and the factors which have to be considered for each of the four categories.

1.1   Placement

A *placement* test is designed to sort new students into teaching groups, so that they can start a course at approximately the same level as the other students in the class. It is concerned with the student's present standing, and so relates to general ability rather than specific points of learning. As a rule the results are needed quickly so that teaching may begin. This puts a severe constraint upon the types of test that can be used. At the same time a variety of tests is necessary because a range of different activities is more likely to give an accurate overall picture of a student's level than a single assessment.

Figure 1   A framework for language assessments

category	content	purpose	considerations
placement	general reference forward to future learning	grouping	speed of results variety of tests interview
diagnostic	detailed reference back to classwork	motivation remedial work	short-term objectives new examples of the material taught
achievement	general reference back to course	certification comparison with others at the same stage	decisions about sampling similar material to that taught in new contexts
proficiency	specific purposes reference forward to particular applications of language acquired	evidence of ability to use language in practical situations	definition of operational needs authenticity context strategies for coping

It is also advisable for one member of staff to see each student individually, if only for two or three minutes, before the final class allocation is made. (This is, of course, vital if the course deals primarily with the spoken language.) At this interview the member of staff can coordinate the results of the various tests that the student has just taken, and add some personal notes to the student's file. This procedure has several advantages. It helps to complete the assessment for each individual student by disclosing factors which are not revealed by the written tests, either positive ones such as a friendly, outgoing character or a higher level of production than a writing test suggests, or negative ones such as a slight stammer or more than average shyness. Also, it establishes each student right from the start of his course as an individual, not just a name and number in the filing system. At a practical level, the interview can sort out minor problems related to application forms and registration procedures. This provides a genuine purpose for the use of the spoken language, which achieves its own end while giving the 'examiner' material on which to assess the student's oral capability.

Perhaps the greatest advantage of the interview is that there is now the opportunity to assess both oral production (the ability to make English sounds) and fluency (the ability to sound English in a social situation) at one and the same time.

1.2 Diagnostic

A *diagnostic* test (sometimes called a *formative* or *progress* test) checks on students' progress in learning particular elements of the course. It is used for example at the end of a unit in the course-book or after a lesson designed to teach one particular point. These tests can take the form of an extension of the lesson from a practice phase into an assessment phase. Carefully organised, however, they can provide information about progress which may be used systematically for remedial work. The diagnostic test tries to answer the question: 'How well have the students learnt this particular material?' Since it relates to particular elements in the course which have just been taught, for example 'type 3 conditional sentences with *if*' or 'asking permission', the assessment will give immediate feedback to the student. If his learning has been successful, the results will give a considerable lift to the student's morale and he is likely to approach the next learning tasks with fresh enthusiasm. If he finds he has not mastered the point at issue, the test should give him clear indications of how he falls short, so that he can do some useful revision. The demands for this kind of test are therefore that it must relate to specific short-term objectives and that it should include further examples of the same kind of material as that used in teaching.

1.3 Achievement

An *achievement* test (also called an *attainment* or *summative* test) looks back over a longer period of learning than the diagnostic test, for example a year's work, or a whole course, or even a variety of different courses. It is intended to show the standard which the students have now reached in relation to other students at the same stage. This standard may be worldwide, as with the Cambridge examinations in EFL; or established for a country, as with school-leaving certificates; or it may relate to an individual school or group of schools which issues certificates to students attending courses. But the important point which is common to all these situations is that the standard remains constant as far as possible from course to course and from year to year and is external to the individual class or textbook. The conditions for setting an achievement test are that it covers a much wider range of material than a diagnostic test and relates to long-term rather than short-term objectives. This brings up problems of sampling, since what has been learnt in a year (for example) cannot all be assessed in one day, yet the test must reflect the content of the whole course. Decisions therefore have to be made about what should be included in the test, and whether assessing one thing can be assumed to include another. For example, if a student can cope with the form and meaning of the past perfect tense, does this imply a similar mastery of the present perfect, since the normal sequence of learning deals with the second of these before the first? On a wider scale, if the student has learnt to write a business letter, can it be assumed that he can cope with personal letters too, on the same basis of the normal sequence of learning?

1.4 Proficiency

The aim of a *proficiency* test is to assess the student's ability to apply in actual situations what he has learnt. It seeks to answer the question: 'Having learnt this much, what can the student do with it?' This type of test is not usually related to any particular course because it is concerned with the student's current standing in relation to his future needs. In view of this future orientation, a proficiency test is the most suitable vehicle for assessing English for Specific Purposes (ESP). However, the purposes for which it serves as an appropriate testing instrument extend far beyond those which are normally cited as 'specific purpose' (such as language for business, for engineers, or for postgraduate study). The language needs of any student will be to some extent specific, even if his intention is no more than to use the language as a tourist. In all these cases, efforts must be made to use in the test the kind of language which actually occurs in the situations the student will meet. For example, a test which sets out to assess the proficiency of a student hoping to follow a university course in an English-speaking country would need to take into account not only his level of skills in listening to lectures, but also his ability to take notes, to make full use of what is written on the blackboard or projected, and finally to use the information he has gained from the lecture in his subsequent writing. An important element in proficiency testing is to assess in some way the student's ability to repair breakdowns in communication, by asking for a repetition or an explanation, for example, or by apologising and rephrasing what he has just tried to say.

This division of tests into separate categories is clearly rather arbitrary, and though it is convenient to say that the purpose of any test can be defined in this way, there are in practice several different purposes for every test. For example, it has been argued above that an achievement test assesses the learning that has gone before, and is therefore concerned with the past, but a student taking this kind of test usually does so because he needs the qualification to convince someone else of his future potential, either as a student in a more advanced course or as an employee.

In the same way, although a proficiency test is not in theory concerned with how the student's present stage of competence has been arrived at, he may well have prepared for it by taking a course designed to help him to pass.

The four types of test described above form the basis for the central part of this book, Chapters 4–7, in which techniques for setting tests are given in detail. Before these practical issues are reached, however, there follows a discussion of the fundamental qualities required in good language tests of all kinds.

2 Qualities of a good test

The three most important characteristics of a good test are reliability, validity and practicality. These abstract nouns may seem rather daunting, but just as it is impossible to play chess without knowing how a knight moves across the board, so it is pointless to try to write tests without a basic understanding of the principles behind them. A teacher who is unaware of the relationship between the content of a test and the consistency of its results is in danger of writing tests which produce misleading information about his students.

2.1 Reliability

The *reliability* of a test is its consistency. There would be little point in trying to measure people's waists with a piece of elastic. What is needed is a tape measure which stays the same length all the time, so that one person's waist is known to be eighty-one centimetres and another's ninety-one centimetres. Tests should not be elastic in their measurements: if a student takes a test at the beginning of a course and again at the end, any improvement in his score should be the result of differences in his skills and not inaccuracies in the test. In the same way, it is important that the student's score should be the same (or as nearly as possible the same) whether he takes one version of a test or another (for waist measurements, the same result should be obtained whichever tape measure is used), and whether one person marks the test or another (whoever uses the tape measure). Reliability also means the consistency with which a test measures the same thing all the time (the tape measure should be placed so that it goes round people's waists, not round their hips or the waistband of the trousers they are wearing).

There are therefore three aspects to reliability: the circumstances in which the test is taken, the way in which it is marked and the uniformity of the assessment it makes.

2.2 Validity

The *validity* of a test is the extent to which the test measures what it is intended to measure. There are many different kinds of validity, but only two are vital for the teacher setting his own tests: content validity and face validity.

Content validity is concerned with what goes into the test. The content of a test should be decided by considering the purposes of the assessment, and then drawn up as a list known as a content specification.* The content specification is important because it ensures as far as possible that the test reflects all the areas to be assessed in suitable proportions and also because it represents a balanced sample, without bias towards the kinds of items which are easiest to write or towards the test material which happens to be available.

Face validity is concerned with what teachers and students think of the test. Does it appear to them a reasonable way of assessing the students, or does it seem trivial, or too difficult, or unrealistic? The only way to find out about face validity is to ask the teachers and students concerned for their opinions, either formally by means of a questionnaire or informally by discussion in class or staff room.

The relationship between reliability and validity is rather complex. On the one hand, a test can be reliable without being valid. For example, a multiple-choice test of individual vocabulary items could be a highly reliable measure because it produced consistent results in the senses explained above, but it would not be a valid measure if it were taken to indicate the students' capacity to understand a text which included the same words, or their ability to use the words productively.

A test cannot be valid, however, without also being reliable. An uncontrolled speaking test, in which a student talked about nothing in particular and was graded on the teacher's spontaneous reactions, would not produce useful results, because there would be no basis for comparison between one student and another, one assessor and another, or one occasion and another. A grade B awarded for a 'test' like this would not mean much, because the student had not been given enough guidance on what to say, and the assessor had no consistent basis for judgement.

2.3 Practicality

The main questions of *practicality* are administrative. Just as a teacher cannot be effective without some forward planning (if only to ensure that a cassette recorder will be available and in working order for his lesson), a test must be well organised in advance. How long will the test take? What special arrangements have to be made (for example what happens to the rest of the class while individual speaking tests take place)? Is any equipment needed (tape recorder, language laboratory, overhead projector)? How long will it take to get the marking done, and how many people will be involved (teacher time is a hidden expense)? How will test materials be reproduced in quantity, and at what cost, and how will they be stored between sittings of the test (security may be important)? What arrangements can be made for efficient filing of test materials, so that teachers can easily find what they want?

In brief, tests should be as economical as possible in time (preparation, sitting and marking) and in cost (materials and hidden costs of time spent). This sounds a very obvious statement to make, but it is easy to lose sight of overall efficiency in the detailed work required to prepare appropriate and useful tests.

2.4 Comparison and discrimination

Finally, a discussion of the basic concepts behind testing would be incomplete without treating the closely related ideas of *comparison* and *discrimination*. In a sense, all assessment is based on comparison, either between one student and another, or between the student as he is now and as he was earlier, or between the student's capability and the task the test requires him to perform. Comparisons between two sets of scores obtained for the same group of students are the basis of estimates of reliability. This means that test results are relative, and a score has no absolute value beyond the context in which it was obtained.

This is true both for small scale tests and for large scale examinations. A student who gets a score of 75 per cent on a classroom test seems to have done well, but his result is less impressive if twenty of the twenty-five students in his class achieve higher scores. Alternatively, a score of 30 per cent could be the highest in the class. These two cases may be considered extreme, but the principle they illustrate is that scores from different tests should not be assumed to have equivalent value and so should not be added together unless they have roughly the same spread of marks.

The authority of an external examination like the Cambridge First Certificate is the outcome of its stability over many years and many thousands of candidates, whose scores have all contributed to establishing the standard of the examination. Any new candidate's performance is in effect compared with the performances of all his predecessors. If the scores on a large scale examination such as this were drawn as a graph, they would tend to look like *a* in Figure 2. This is because the largest number of scores would occur at or near the middle of the range and the better and worse scores would become fewer towards each end.

A distribution* of this shape is likely to appear if random measurements, for example the height of all the adult women in London, are drawn up as a graph. This shape, the 'normal' curve*, is a fiction, because it will not occur exactly in practice, but it is useful as a constant yardstick against which to judge the reliability of test results. It also gives a basis for the calculation of discrimination*, which is the extent to which a test separates the students from each other.

Figure 2   Distributions

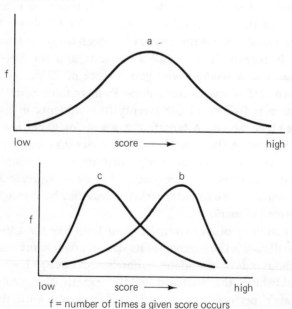

f = number of times a given score occurs

A curve of this type, however, is not necessarily the distribution which every kind of test should aim to produce. An achievement test should result in a wide spread of scores because it is then easier to make decisions about where to separate one group of students from another so that they can be awarded different grades. In the same way, the more efficiently a placement test discriminates between students, the easier it is to divide them into teaching groups. In both cases, a regular distribution (like the normal one) is appropriate. A diagnostic test, however, may be intended to show that nearly all students have learnt the material tested, and in this case they should all get fairly high scores, so that the graph drawn for this test would look more like *b* in Figure 2. Moving the mountain to the right in this way, that is to the upper end of the distribution, is 'negative skew'. From the point of view of the students and the teacher, this is excellent: it shows that most of the students have learnt what the teacher has been trying to teach them, and that only a few of them need to do revision or remedial work. A normal curve would imply that the test was not a good one for diagnostic purposes.

There is a more general point involved, too. If the distribution is skewed, either negatively or positively (*c* in Figure 2), the usual judgements about reliability, based on calculations relating to the normal distribution, cannot be made because they assume a regular curve of a standard kind, spread out along the range of marks in a symmetrical way.

The intention of this chapter has been to introduce the concepts necessary for the discussion of assessment purposes and test types which follows. Chapters 4–7 will show how they should be taken into account in the setting of tests. In Chapters 8 and 9 they will be taken up again in more detail and applied to test scores, so that judgements can be made about what the results mean for the students, how accurate the test was and how it can be improved for future sittings.

3 Test design

The writing of a successful test begins with a specification, and the more accurately this can be drawn up the better. Unfortunately, so many factors have to be taken into account in the process that assumptions have to be made at every stage. A good specification is therefore the result of careful judgements rather than precise definitions.

The model given in Figure 3 is one which teachers can use to draw up their own specifications. Those suggested in Chapters 4–7 are unlikely to be relevant in every case, since each test writer has to decide what to put in the specification to achieve his own particular aims. He does this on the strength of his teaching experience and knowledge of the circumstances in which the test is to be used. Only he can judge when to amend or ignore factors which have been included in the sample specifications and when to add others.

3.1 Outline for a specification

OBJECTIVES

What is written under this heading on a test specification depends on the kind of test the teacher is designing. For a placement test, the reference is forward to the demands the course will make. It might seem logical, therefore, to set tests relating to students' future learning by setting up negative targets like 'Cannot yet cope with course content from Unit 12 onwards'. But a placement

Figure 3   Elements in a specification

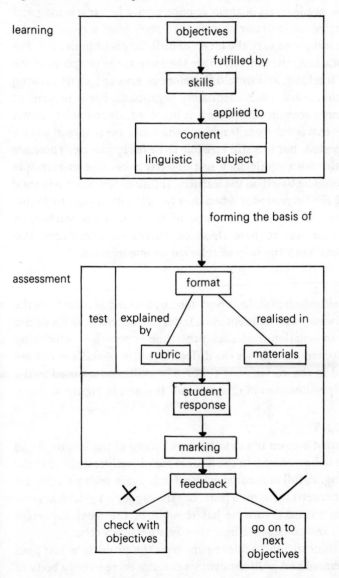

test is taken by all levels of students, and a test which aimed to meet the needs of all of them at once would be far too long and complicated. It is better therefore to start from a more general content and try to vary the levels of difficulty within the test. For diagnostic tests the objectives are the same as the purposes of the current teaching, and should therefore be easy to specify (as long as the course has been adequately organised). For achievement tests a more complicated process is involved, since the objectives must be extracted from teaching which has been spread over a longer period, but it is still possible to be fairly precise. There are difficulties with proficiency test objectives because in principle they should be based on the learners' future needs (what will they be using the language for when they have learnt it?) and to do this thoroughly is beyond the scope of the individual teacher. In practice, he has to base these objectives on experience and judgement, with the help of relevant course material.

SKILLS
The specification of skills is best done by looking at them from the point of view of the student as he takes the test. Since skills do not operate in isolation from each other, the approach to specifying them adopted here shows the different groups of skills which are involved in the various test types. The skills coding used in the sample specifications in Chapters 4–7 is given in Figure 4.

CONTENT
The content section is a detailed breakdown of the language and subjects to be covered, in the light of the objectives defined at the beginning. A full content specification is again impracticable for the teacher setting his own tests, but the suggested guidelines will help him to make sure he has thought of the most important elements and considered how they relate to each other.

For diagnostic and achievement tests the problem is less than for placement and proficiency tests because there exists a body of

Figure 4 Skills coding for specifications*

code	language	skill	receptive	productive	psycho-logical	content
L S R W	1 = native language 2 = target language	listen speak read write	√ √	 √ √		
v		interpret visuals (pictures, diagrams)	√			
e		apply expectancy grammar+			√	
c		show knowledge of content				√
t		mark answer mechanically (by tick or letter code)		√		
a		act		√		
d		draw		√		
s		summarise		√		

*Italics are used in the specifications to indicate the principal skills assessed for each test.
†See Glossary.

material which is to be sampled for the test. The teacher's book of a well organised course will provide an excellent basis, but for the achievement test other material used in the course may need to be sampled as well.

FORMAT
It is important that the mechanics of the test should be considered at an early stage, so that the implications can be taken into account and major revisions later on can be avoided. Under this heading come length of reading or listening text, number of questions, use of recording, use of multiple-choice or other objective techniques, length of time allowed for the test and so on.

RUBRIC
The instructions given to the student on how he is to do the test are a very important aspect of validity. The wording has to be carefully chosen, especially at the lower levels, and if all the students have the same native language it may well be worth using it for clarity's sake. These explanations are less crucial if the test follows the familiar form of a class exercise, as it might in a diagnostic or achievement test. However, if it is new to the students, as for example with a placement test, the teacher should try to make sure before the test begins that all the students know what to do. Examples of test items should usually be given as part of the rubric, but may be omitted if the test follows a teaching procedure which the students know well. The rubric can also be understood in a wider sense to mean all the arrangements made by the test setter to enable the student to give his attention to the content rather than the form of a test. In this definition, it is a failure of rubric when the pauses on the tape in a listening test are not long enough for the students to answer the questions, or when the passage for reading is continued on the back of the test sheet and some of the students do not realise it. The result of inadequate rubrics is that the marker cannot tell from the student's answer whether he has the required skill or not.

MATERIALS

This is a question of administration, but again needs considering at a fairly early stage. Of primary interest are any facilities which may be usefully exploited (for example, duplication, photocopying, overhead projector). At this point too it is useful to make a decision about the length of time the test is to be available, and whether it is going to be repeated often enough to make it worthwhile producing the set of tests in booklet form.

The differing circumstances in which tests can be taken affect the test materials used considerably. A formal test (usually achievement) requires that the content and marking are kept secure, which is another reason for producing the tests in booklets. The booklets are numbered in a sequence so that any lost will be immediately noticed, students not being allowed to leave the room until all booklets have been collected. The booklets can be used over and over again, since the students answer on separate numbered answer sheets. It may also be necessary to produce several different forms* of a secure test of this kind, so that the content is different at various sittings and any 'leaks' from a student who has taken the test to another who is yet to take it will be of no value. A completely new content may not be essential; it is usually sufficient to include some new material and alter the order of the rest. Changing the keys of multiple-choice tests by shuffling the order of the options can be a very effective security measure.

An informal test will usually be taken in class under normal class conditions. It is best produced as one or several separate sheets which the student can keep for class discussion and future reference and revision. (This may be encouraged by punching two holes in the sheets in advance so that they can be kept in a ring file.)

The reproduction of test materials is a question of quantity in relation to cost and of both in relation to quality. The importance of a formal test probably requires it to look impressive or as well produced as circumstances allow, which for large numbers could mean printing by lithography or (less expensively) duplicating by waxed stencil. Spirit duplication is suitable only for informal class tests, especially since the number of copies from one master is quite limited. Photocopying is probably too expensive except for small numbers, but may be necessary for visual material where detail is important. In this case, if cost is an important consideration, the copies can be collected in rather than kept by the students, since on their own visuals are of little use in the file.

MARKING

It is easy to assume, particularly with objective tests, that the marking can safely be left until the tests have been taken, but problems may well arise which could have been sorted out earlier or which, in some cases, could have been avoided completely. Both the layout of the answer sheet and the instructions on it for students are important. If there are a large number of items in an objective test, it is helpful if they are grouped in fives and clearly numbered so that there is less risk of a student filling in a whole series of answers in the wrong places after missing out one item. There should also be provision at the beginning for one or two examples.

The marking of subjective tests needs considerable thought in advance, partly because the system used depends on the aims and content of the test, and partly because time may have to be allowed both for pretesting and for standardising markers afterwards. It is very important that the practical issues of marking (how it will be done, who will do it and how long it will take) should be taken into account as part of the setting of the test, and not as an afterthought.

The balance of the different tests in the final results, or weighting, should also be considered at the specification stage, to ensure that it reflects the intentions of the assessment as a whole.

At the end of the procedure of drawing up the specification, or perhaps after a few days, it is advisable to go back over it and try to justify every decision. This will give an overall perspective and bring out any contradictions which were not noticed during the detailed work on each section. (This kind of review is also very helpful after setting the tests themselves.)

The next four chapters contain sample specifications for four batteries* of tests: placement, diagnostic, achievement and proficiency. Each of these specifications is accompanied by a review of the relevant concepts from Chapter 2, and a commentary. This is followed by practical suggestions for setting the tests and finally references to other test types which might be used for similar purposes. The intention is to provide, by means of examples, a framework into which teachers can slot their own material.

A list of all the tests discussed in the next four chapters is given at the front of the book. For ease of reference, each of them has been identified by one of the letters A–Z. Also, each test has been graded in terms of its suitability for the various testing purposes.

4 Placement tests

4.1 Review

It was argued in Chapter 1 that the contents of a placement test should be general, referring forward to the course the student is going to take, and that important conditions are speed of results and the use of a variety of tests, including an interview. In the light of Chapter 2 it can be added that the tests should spread the students out over a wide range of scores so that they can be sorted as efficiently as possible into class groups. The need for the assessment to be general (rather than specific to previous teaching) means that it could be based on some or all of the following: information or narration (with understanding checked by true/false items), integrative tests such as cloze or dictation, something written, and something spoken. Further details of these test types are given in the specification (Figure 5) and explained in the commentary section which follows.

Figure 5   Placement tests: a specification

Objectives
1   to assess the level of the student's general language ability, if possible in terms of the course he is going to take
2   to place the student on a scale in relation to other students so that he can be given appropriate teaching

Skills†

test A: *L2*/R2/t scripted speech
test B: *R2*/t narrative text

	test C:	R2/*W2* structured writing
alternatives	test D:	*R2*/W2/*e* cloze
	test E:	*L2*/W2/*e* dictation
	test F:	L2/*S2* conversation

Content

language: a variety of everyday vocabulary; structures not beyond Alexander *et al* 1975 Stage IIi or similar; A, B, E and F becoming more difficult towards the end

subjects: common human experience, avoiding culture bias; learning context (including strategies for class exchanges); student's own experience

Formats

	test A:	listening text, 400 words (3 minutes) + 15 items, T/F (15 minutes)
	test B:	reading text, 250 words + 20 items, T/F (30 minutes)
	test C:	short stimulus, write about own experience (15 minutes)
alternatives	test D:	cloze text, 400 words, gaps every 9th, 40 items (30 minutes)
	test E:	dictation, 150 words (15 minutes)
	test F:	conversation, 15 items from list of 25 (5 minutes)
		total test time: 60 or 75 minutes + 5 minutes each student (test F)

Rubrics as simple as possible; examples essential; teacher introduces; in students' native language if practical

Materials

student: stencilled sheets/booklet; answer sheet

teacher: Tape of scripted speech and playback equipment; text of dictation; list of questions for conversation; key and marking schemes; scoring sheets (1 per student for conversation)

Marking

	test A:	30 marks (15 items x 2)
	test B:	20 marks (20 items x 1)
	test C:	20 marks (see chapter 8)
alternatives	test D:	20 marks (40 items x ½)
	test E:	20 marks (see chapter 8)
	test F:	30 marks (15 items x 2)
		(total marks: 100)

---

† for key to coding of skills, see Figure 4, page 19.

4.2 Commentary

The circumstances in which placement tests are used require that they should be relatively formal, but given in a relaxed atmosphere. However, since the results are important, and since there may be an unusual amount of nervousness at this first meeting which begins a new course, both the student and the teacher (but particularly the student) are likely to be under considerable pressure. This pressure will be reduced by friendliness on the part of the teacher and explanations of what is going to happen. The tests themselves should be fairly short, so that they do not take too long to answer or to mark. In this case, however, they will not be reliable enough individually and the results should be added together to form a general assessment.

This general assessment is usually all that is needed for a placement test, but in some circumstances, for instance when the student is starting an ESP course, it may be possible to specify more exactly what the course will contain and so assess the student's level in each part of it. However, this would mean that each component test should be longer. There is no point in separating the tests in this way, of course, unless something positive is done with the results, such as organising different class groupings for different parts of the course. This involves complex organisation and aspects of course design which are beyond the scope of this book.

The objectives in the specification are rather different from those for other kinds of test, because placement tests cannot be geared to the learning which went before. A more accurate heading might be 'aims', which are usually considered to be more general than objectives. A placement test 'objective' would have to be worded something like 'can cope with the level taught in class X (or class Y, or class Z)', which is not very helpful without some account of what goes on in these classes.

All four of the main language skills (listening, reading, writing and speaking) should be tested, and in addition, 'expectancy' (see glossary). For tests which require the student to write, alternatives have been suggested. One reason for this is that less is to be expected in this skill from some students than from others (especially from those whose native language is written in non-roman script), particularly at pre-intermediate levels. On the other hand, one of the alternatives may be more closely related to the course which is to follow. Another reason is that a teacher may be happier with one test type rather than another (which is why alternatives are given in all the specifications). Naturally, all the tests could be used, or none of them, depending on the teacher's judgement of what is appropriate to the circumstances.

The language content of placement tests cannot be specified in detail because it must be suitable for a wide range of students with different learning backgrounds. The range of the students' experience is one of level as well as content, and since the intention is to separate them out into class groups, it is useful to set the tests, where possible, on an 'incline of difficulty'. This means that a test starts at a fairly easy level and then gets more and more difficult as it continues. The main advantage of this procedure is that it provides something for students of all levels within a single test. For students at the lower levels, the sticking point may come fairly near the beginning, whereas higher level students will be able to pass quickly through the easiest parts and may not need to think hard until much later on. Of the tests discussed in this chapter, an incline of difficulty can be applied to *A: scripted speech* and *B: narrative*. It can also be used in *E: dictation* and the fifteen questions in *F: conversation*.

'Common human experience' (family, work, eating, sleeping . . .) is suggested in the specification as the basis for subject matter because this is all that can be assumed for every student and, more importantly, because it sets the tests in a personal context which makes it easier for the student to write something (*C: structured writing*) and say something (*F: conver-*

sation). In the case of *C: structured writing* there are other advantages: for example, it makes it clear that the writing does not have to be a formal essay (with beginning, middle and end), which would be too difficult for the weaker student and too academic a test for most placement purposes; and it may incidentally give teachers helpful information about the individual student. Language used in learning (formulation of questions, asking for information or repetition, understanding instructions) is another area of common ground and also a help in assessing the student's level.

The use of a single connected text for *A: scripted speech* and *B: narrative* (rather than several short separate ones) is justified partly because a connected context is easier for the student to follow and partly because a variety of items* at different levels of difficulty can be written on different aspects of a comparatively short connected text. True/false items are easier (and so quicker) to write than multiple-choice items, and have a more direct relationship with the text. If the students all have the same native language, it is worth considering writing the items in that language rather than in the foreign language, but this alters the balance of the test (for example by making it easier, allowing more complex wording of items and affecting the time to be allowed). The short stimulus for *C: structured writing* is intended to leave the writing task relatively free, since a general assessment is all that is required. Again, the stimulus could be given in the native language if it is common to all candidates.

There is a considerable problem with the rubrics for placement tests, unless they too are written in the students' native language. Some of the students may have little understanding of the foreign language (though presumably teachers will know in advance which students are absolute beginners and will not expect them to take placement tests). Also, the test formats may all be new to the students, without the necessary connection with previous class-work procedures that there is in diagnostic and achievement tests.

The suggestion therefore is that the teacher administering the test goes through the rubrics carefully with each group to make sure that as far as possible all the students have understood what they are to do. This may add to the time taken for the tests, but it is well worth the extra effort.

If the placement test battery is to be used fairly often it may be worthwhile to reproduce it in the form of a booklet, with a separate answer sheet. This takes longer to prepare but is more economical in the long run because it means that the booklets can be used over and over again and only the answer sheet needs to be produced in large quantities. Also, as mentioned in the last chapter, this system helps to keep the tests secure: it is much more difficult to keep control of separate test sheets than it is to issue and collect test booklets, especially if the booklets are numbered in an unbroken series. (In this case any booklet damaged or written on is replaced for the next sitting with a new copy bearing the same number.)

The use of tape recordings for tests involving listening has advantages and disadvantages. In the case of *A: scripted speech* it is suggested that the text is recorded because this makes the test more authentic, as if the students were actually listening to a radio talk or telephone message. It also means that the test is more reliable because all students hear exactly the same text throughout all repeats and at all sittings of the test. On the other hand, it is suggested that the text for *E: Dictation* should be read by the teacher because this humanises the procedure. It is reassuring to students to know that the person dictating can see when they have finished writing and will adjust the pauses accordingly (within limits), and that interruptions or noise can be allowed for. Pauses of fixed length on a tape can cause students to hurry and may put unnecessary pressure on them as they write. Because of this personal contact between teacher and students it is probably best, if a dictation is to be included, to put it first in the sequence of tests.

A completely different approach to placement testing suitable for language schools and other institutions in which English is the language of administration is to use for assessment purposes the physical procedure through which the student must pass on his first day at the school. For example, he must at some stage have his name checked against a list of expected arrivals; he will probably be given both written and spoken instructions about the day's procedures, the school and the course; and he will need to find his way to various places in the school building. These can all be used as a basis for assessment and build up like tests into a collection of useful information. Some safeguards are needed, however, to ensure that no student can bypass the procedure. A typical example of an entry procedure geared towards placement might be:

1 registration at reception desk, student says who he is, receives registration form and written information about the day's events/the course/the school/the town/accommodation arranged;
2 student goes to designated classroom, fills in registration form (including short personal statement);
3 introductory talk from a member of staff about the school/course (link with written material received earlier);
4 individual interview with a teacher who checks verbally with the student the information he has given on his form (which teacher retains), briefly checks also on the student's understanding of the procedures explained in the talk, and makes a coordinated assessment of the student's level on the basis of all he has done.

All these stages in the entry procedure allow for assessment of language used for a practical purpose: the needs of the student at the time. If teachers feel that a better safeguard than the final interview is required, or if time cannot be found for the full interview as suggested above, one of the tests (probably *D: cloze*) could be taken by all students, possibly between stages 3 and 4 in the above procedure.

4.3 Setting the tests

A: SCRIPTED SPEECH
Text
The difference between scripted speech and unscripted speech arises from the circumstances in which it is spoken. A radio play, a news broadcast and a weather report are scripted; a conversation and a discussion are unscripted. But the distinction is not always so clear-cut. A lecturer may speak from notes; the topics for discussion in a radio programme may have been rehearsed, or the recording of it edited before it is broadcast; a politician may alter his speech from the script handed out in advance to the newspapers.

In tests, the same kind of variation can result. For example, the conversation in *M: unscripted speech* was originally spontaneous, but for testing purposes it needed to be rerecorded on the basis of a transcript (see page 69). The talk for *N: unscripted speech* is given from a diagram (page 75) and the lecture in *T: transfer* is made from notes (page 95). The texts for *G* and *H* (both *scripted speech*) are manufactured, that is, written specially for the purpose, the former by the test setter (page 54) and the latter by a course book writer (page 56).

In the case of *A: scripted speech* (Figure 6) the text is an edited version of a newspaper article resulting from an interview. The article itself was probably written with the help of a tape recording.

This text was chosen because it consists of the kind of language which appears in radio talks, and in addition it has the personal, day-to-day content required by the specification. Other ways of obtaining scripted texts are to record from radio broadcasts or the telephone (although this may involve legal problems); to make notes of broadcasts and reconstruct a text from them; to base the text on short excerpts from modern plays (though passages have to be chosen with care); or perhaps the simplest method, to take or adapt listening material from course books, often with the added advantage of a ready-made recording. Many of the listening texts used in courses, however, are not scripted speech in the sense in which the term is used here, since they are tidy versions of unscripted speech which have been invented to illustrate a teaching point. But circumstances may not require (or even allow) authenticity to be insisted on to this extent.

Figure 6   Test A: scripted speech – text

Day in the life of a musician

At home in Switzerland I get up about 7 or 7.30 – depends when the children get up. They attack my wife Margaret and me – our bed's like a rugby field. * Some days I have porridge for breakfast, some days an orange, sometimes nothing. I don't see the point of doing the same thing every day. After Peter goes to school I start work in the music room, but I don't practise for a set number of hours. When I don't feel like playing any more I go for a walk in the hills or I read. * I have a very simple lunch at about half past twelve, perhaps a sleep afterwards or a coffee by the lake. The ideal afternoon would be sunshine, go swimming with the children, take them all into town for a hamburger, chips and a Coke. * There's usually something going on in the evening, but Margaret and I like to reserve one evening a week just for ourselves. We don't have big parties except for a real celebration at Christmas. * I don't get very drunk: alcohol doesn't affect me like it does other people. I prefer beer to wine, but it has a disastrous effect on the figure. I know it's fashionable to be thin but I'm not really a fashionable person . . .*

(the next 150 words of this text have been omitted)

. . . Sometimes I listen to music just for pleasure. The other day I heard old Horowitz playing his tune, you know, that Rachmaninov thing. I listen a tremendous amount to John Denver. He's a sort of musical millionaire. There's a sort of happiness about his singing. But I'll be glad to get back home.

---

* indicates a break between sections

The text in Figure 6 is in any case only an imitation, since it was not originally a radio talk, but at least it is an account of what was really said on an actual occasion. The extent to which the published text has been edited for assessment purposes is shown by this extract from it, which can be compared with the text in Figure 6.

'At home in Lucerne I get up about 7 or 7.30 – depends when the kids get up. They attack you – our bed's like a rugby field. Some days I have porridge for breakfast, some days an orange, sometimes nothing. I don't see the point of doing the same thing every day. After Paddy (the eldest, aged seven) disappears to school I start work in the studio, but I don't practise for a set number of hours. I just noodle around till I get fed up. If I don't feel like playing, I take off for the hills or I read . . .'

The amendments are more frequent at the beginning of the text than at the end because it is important to start at a relatively low level, and particularly in this case because of the intention to set the test on an incline of difficulty (see page 27).

Repetitions and sections
The next step is to decide whether, and if so how often, the text is to be repeated, and whether it should be broken up into sections. The authentic procedure for a test of scripted speech would be for the students to hear the text once, as they would in real life. In a placement test, the students are new to the testing system and so need all possible help and guidance in following the test procedure. This suggests that the text should be given in sections and repeated, so that the test does not over-extend the student's memory or his tolerance of his own inability to understand all that he hears.

This division of the text into sections can cause problems for the content of items. There are several ways of relating the items to the text. A helpful method is for the test setter to make notes on the important points of the text as he listens to it, so that he works from an outline of the content based on an understanding of the passage as it is heard. If the test writer has already edited the text, however, he may be too familiar with it by now to be able to take notes only from what he hears. It is better for him then to leave it for a few days and come back fresh to the note taking, or better still, to ask someone else to take the notes. Another method is to use a written version (either the original if the text has been invented or a transcript if the original was in fact spoken). Unfortunately, however, looking at a written version tends to suggest ideas for items which are based on a visual appreciation of the text rather than an aural one, particularly details which can be referred to again in a text that is read but which are lost in a text that is heard. Once the items have been written it is well worth checking back over them to make sure that they all depend on listening rather than reading.

The text should be divided into roughly equal sections according to the number of items to be written, but allowing a section at the beginning for examples and reserving the last two or three items for more general reference, either to several sections or to the text as a whole. In Figure 6 each break between sections is indicated by an asterisk (*). The first section is used for the two examples, and the last two items, 14 and 15, refer to the whole text rather than the last section of it. This system also ensures that the items follow the order of the text.

Items
There are two basic rules for writing true/false items. Firstly, the statements should be as short and simple as possible because they are not the main target of the assessment, only a way into the text and a means of investigating the student's understanding. Secondly, negative statements should be avoided because the student is likely to be confused by the resulting double negatives (for example, 'He does not have the same breakfast every day'.

Figure 7   Test A: scripted speech – true/false items

Example 1 His home is in Switzerland.	☑
Example 2 His wife's name is Mary.	☒
1 He has the same breakfast every day.	☐
2 He practises in the mornings.	☐
3 Lunch is at 12.30.	☐
4 They live in the middle of the town.	☐
5 They have a party one evening every week.	☐
6 He wants to be thin.	☐
(six items omitted)	
13 The 'thing' is a piece of music.	☐
14 He works harder in England than in Switzerland.	☐
15 His concerts are all in London.	☐

Student's response: 'Yes, it is true that he does not . . .' or 'No, it is not true that he does not . . .').

Some test writers add a third possibility to the simple true/false judgement: 'The text does not tell us . . .' (not necessarily in this wording). This takes the item halfway towards a multiple-choice format and reduces the chances of right answers resulting from guessing.

The value of a true/false item for assessment purposes, whether it relates to a spoken or to a written text, lies in how accurately it demonstrates that a particular process of understanding has taken place. Some of the various possibilities for demanding different kinds of understanding are illustrated in Figure 7. Example 1 and Example 2 are factual, whereas Item 4 depends on an inference (a wrong one which is disproved by 'take them all into town', supported by 'walk in the hills'). Item 3 has short reference (to 'lunch at about half past twelve') but Item 14 refers to the whole text. Item 6 explores the viewpoint of the speaker. These demands, however, cannot be made individually by different items, and it is clear that Examples 1 and 2 are also short-reference items and Item 6 depends on an inference. But all of them relate to contextual meaning rather than to separate points of meaning or structure. It would be inappropriate for example to include in this test the item 'Porridge is a soft food of boiled oatmeal'. It can be answered without reference to the passage at all, and there are better ways of assessing vocabulary (see page 58).

Rubric

After the items have been written, the next step is to work out the rubric. This should contain an introduction to the content of the test, full instructions for doing it and examples of items. It is helpful to the students if the rubric appears in writing at the top of the page of items as well as in a spoken introduction to the text. The combination of spoken and written instructions establishes the speed and rhythm of the whole test so that students know what to expect from the tape or reader. For instance, in Figure 8 there are two examples because each section of text has two items relating to it. After the text has been heard right through once it is useful to allow a little time for the students to scan the items so that they have some idea of the extent of the test and can begin to listen in the sections for specific information. It is also a good idea to add a rubric at the bottom of the page which again echoes the spoken instructions at the end so that the test is seen as a logical whole.

Recording

It was suggested earlier that this test should be recorded if possible. This does not necessarily require the use of a recording studio and professional help, though if they are available it would obviously be sensible to take advantage of them. More important

Figure 8   Test A: scripted speech – rubrics

A: Listen to this radio talk. It is about a day in the life of a musician. You will hear it three times altogether. First, listen to all of it.

B: At home . . . back home.

A: That is the end of the talk. Now open your test book and look at the statements for this test.
PAUSE 30 SECONDS

A: Now you will hear the talk again, with pauses which will give you time to write your answers. Each statement is either right or wrong about what the speaker has said. If it is right, put a tick (√) in the box, and if it is wrong, put a cross (x) in the box.
Here are two examples.

B: At home . . . . . rugby field.

A: Examples 1 and 2: are they right or wrong?
PAUSE 10 SECONDS

A: Example 1 was right and Example 2 was wrong, so there is a tick in the first box and a cross in the second. Now listen to the first section.

B: Some days . . . . . or I read.

A: Statements 1 and 2: are they right or wrong?
PAUSE 10 SECONDS

A: Now listen to the next section.
. . . (continued) . . .

A: That is the end of the test.

---

than ideal acoustic conditions for the recording are the quality of the tape recorder (which should be the best available), consistency in the speed of delivery, and reasonably accurate timing of pauses (an ordinary watch showing seconds is quite adequate for this). It is best if two people can do the recording, one to read the rubrics and the other to read the text. This contrast of voices makes the test easier to follow and more lively.

B: NARRATIVE TEXT

Like *A: scripted speech* this test consists of a text and true/false items so that much of the discussion of the previous section also applies here. The only difference is that since a written text is under the control of the student in a way that a spoken text is not, the items can be more detailed. The principles of reading tests as opposed to listening tests will be considered in connection with test *O: text and argument* (page 76), so that for the present the main questions are: what kind of a test is produced by following the specification and where can suitable texts be found?

A test based on a narrative text is likely to be in a past tense and to include sequence and description. Amongst the items should be some which demand an understanding of these dimensions: statements beginning with 'when . . .', 'after . . .', 'before . . .' or including references to time such as days and dates; and others which include short paraphrases of characteristics of places and people which are either stated or implied by the text.

Examples of reading material suitable for this test are probably the easiest to find of all because they often form the core of textbooks and are used extensively in supplementary comprehension exercises and readers. Structured readers can be particularly useful in test setting. More immediate material may be adapted from human interest stories in newspapers, but the story will often need to be entirely rewritten, especially for tests at the lower levels, because newspaper text is very elliptical. It tends to assume that the reader is used to the style of the paper, has read yesterday's edition and so knows the background to today's news, and is also aware of the cultural significance of its statements.

C: STRUCTURED WRITING
The point of asking the student to write in a placement test is mainly to provide a basis for a general assessment of self expression. However, what he produces must be controlled to a certain extent, and the simplest way is to give him a framework or structure on which to write. For the weaker student, especially one whose native language is written in a non-roman alphabet, it will show how quickly and how legibly he can write, and for the stronger student it will offer a chance to show how appropriately

he can use what he knows for a specified purpose. Some teachers take the view that the writing section of a placement test is only a double check in case of doubt and is not marked otherwise; others scan the writing very rapidly and make a quick judgement on the basis of length achieved (in a given time), legibility of handwriting, and what might be called 'sophistication': the general level at which the student can express himself in writing, looked at from the point of view of content rather than formal correctness (which is assessed elsewhere in the placement battery). Both these approaches seem a little too casual, especially if writing is an important element in the following course, and it is preferable to set up definite categories for the marking (discussed in detail in Chapter 8).

Suitable subjects for the structured writing test (which the specification says should be about the student's own experience) could be the journey to the school for the test, or on an earlier visit; an incident on holiday/at work/at a weekend; accommodation in lodgings, hostel, hall of residence; an accident on the road or in the home; and so on. In each case the rubric should specify who the student is writing for (friend, official, teacher, school administrator) and how long his writing is to be (either by the time allowed or by a number of lines or pages). A very brief outline of content should also be given. Some test writers give the student one or two sentences to start him off in the right direction, which is the equivalent of an example in a test of receptive skills, but this is not essential.

An example of wording (suitable for a course in English for Academic Purposes) is:

'You have 15 minutes for this test.

Write a short report for the university about the Hall you are staying in. Write something about
- the rooms
- the food
- the atmosphere'

D: CLOZE

Principles

The cloze procedure originated in the 1950s as a means of assessing the difficulty of a reading text for native speakers, but within three years its originator was suggesting that it could be used for assessing the progress of second and foreign language learners. The principle is that single words are taken out of a text at regular intervals, leaving gaps which students have to complete with appropriate 'fillers', one only for each gap. In order to do this the student has to refer to the text on either side of the gap so that he can judge what an appropriate filler might be, taking into account both meaning and structure.

There are two types of gap: 'function' gaps (such as conjunctions, prepositions, articles) which have only one correct filler, and 'semantic' gaps (such as nouns, adjectives, verbs, adverbs) that can be filled with any one of a number of alternatives. Even within a restricted context there can be quite a number of semantic fillers, as for example Item 9 in Figure 9, where the original was 'experienced' but 'good', 'talented', 'expert', 'qualified', 'interested', 'our', 'Eurocentre', 'language', among others, could all be considered reasonable.

The variation in acceptable fillers leads to two main systems of marking: 'exact' and 'acceptable'. The first of these means that only the original word is counted as correct, and since there is only one right answer, the marking is objective and can be done quickly, without skilled judgements. In 'acceptable' marking, decisions must be made about whether a student's offering is good enough to be counted as correct or not. Since native speakers will often suggest fillers which are as good as or even better than the original (in the judgement of other native speakers), it seems unfair to insist on the replacement of the exact word. It has been shown, however, that the two systems of marking produce very similar results, in the sense that the students are sorted into

Figure 9 Test D: cloze

You have 30 minutes for this test.
Here is part of a booklet about a group of language schools. Read it through to the end, then start at the beginning and write ONE word for each space. Write on your answer sheet, not in this booklet. The first answer has been written as an example, to show you what to do.

Learn a living language in a lively way

A language consists of more than just grammar and vocabulary. A language is a living thing, because it's people who use it to express themselves. This is .. (example) .. the Eurocentres are situated where living languages are .. 1 ... The Eurocentres are meeting-places for people from all .. 2 .. the world, people of all ages, from different .. 3 .. and with differing outlooks who nevertheless are united .. 4 .. common aims: to learn a new language, discover .. 5 .. horizons, and to develop their understanding of other .. 6 ... Of course, every participant must contribute his or .. 7 .. own motivation and readiness to learn, but in .. 8 .. company of others and with the help of .. 9 .. teachers things go much more easily, and learning .. 10 .. much more fun. In the Eurocentres we teach .. 11 .. practical language of the everyday world. Our carefully .. 12 .. programmes with clear learning objectives help you rapidly .. 13 .. use the new language with confidence and ease. .. 14 .. the time – in and out of school – you .. 15 .. the chance to put the living language into .. 16 ... Learning and living a new language in the .. 17 .. means above all being in daily contact with .. 18 .. cultural traditions and way of life of the .. 19 ... You cease to feel awkward in a foreign .. 20 .. once you begin to understand what people say .. 21 .. what they write – and a real sense of .. 22 .. comes when you can actually begin to express .. 23 .. in an increasingly individual way. Whenever one of .. 24 .. course participants attains this objective, the Eurocentres are .. 25 .. to the aim they have set themselves: the .. 26 .. of worldwide understanding across the boundaries of language .. 27 .. national frontiers ...

(continued up to 40 items; for key see page 43)

roughly the same rank order.* The main difference is that the scores for all students are lower if the exact system is used.

The essence of the original idea of cloze procedure is that it samples the text at random: a word is deleted at regular intervals through the text, every fifth, or every twelfth, or at any interval between these two extremes. (The distance between gaps, as might be expected, affects the difficulty of the test: the closer together they are, the more difficult it is to find an acceptable filler.) This pure version of cloze is rare except in experimental work, because students may be put off by gaps which are unnecessarily difficult to fill, such as names or numbers. Modified versions are therefore better for assessment purposes, particularly since they help to make every gap a useful contribution to the assessment. Normal modification involves adjusting the gaps to avoid these unreasonable difficulties by taking out the following or preceding word instead. But this is not strictly cloze at all. Modifying the procedure in this way reduces the technical precision of the test, which is claimed to be at its most valid and reliable in its pure form.

A more radical type of modification is to choose which words are to be deleted, on the argument that this is a useful way of assessing particular items of vocabulary or points of structure in context (an argument that is supported by the principle that the test writer should specify as precisely as possible what he intends to assess and then find means of assessing it). But if the basis and justification of cloze is a random sampling of language as it is used, choosing the deletions turns it into one of the many varieties of completion test (see, for example, *H: scripted speech* and *J & K: completion*).

Text

The text for the cloze test given in Figure 9 has been taken from the information booklet issued by a group of language schools. It fulfils the content requirement of the specification because it deals with matters which can be expected to be of interest to students entering on a course. The full text is just under 400 words long, which allows forty deletions to be made at nine-word intervals, leaving a paragraph complete at the beginning and using the first deletion for an example. Oller suggests (1979: 365) that the text should be chosen first and the number of words in it divided by fifty (which he sets as the standard number of items for a cloze test) and the deletions made accordingly. But this means that the length of the text is the deciding factor in the difficulty of the test (see above) and it would seem better to take into account more important factors such as the suitability of content, the time available and the balance between the cloze test and any other tests which are to be taken on the same occasion.

The rubric for a cloze test may suggest that the student reads the text right through before he fills in the gaps. Some test writers explain what 'word' means (for example, that 'it's' and 'meeting-places' each count as one word) but this may be more confusing than helpful in a placement test.

Figure 10   Key to cloze

1	spoken	15	have
2	over	16	practice
3	backgrounds	17	Eurocentres
4	in	18	the
5	new	19	people
6	people	20	language
7	her	21	and
8	the	22	achievement
9	experienced	23	yourself
10	is	24	our
11	the	25	closer
12	worked	26	promotion
13	to	27	and
14	all		

(The marking of this cloze test is intended to be by the 'exact' method, since speed of results is important.)

E: DICTATION

The dictation test associates sound and writing and depends on short-term memory. It assesses a variety of language skills all at once. Although this was considered to be a disadvantage when the theory of testing was that each skill should be assessed separately, it is now thought to reflect what happens when language is used for communicative purposes and it is therefore welcomed again. It has the advantage of covering a variety of language skills and yet providing a single correct version, which can make marking quick and accurate. It is included in the placement test battery because of this efficiency and also because it allows personal contact between teacher and students (see page 5).

Suitable texts for dictations used as placement tests are written versions of spoken language such as dialogues, speeches or announcements. (Any text can of course be dictated but the more characteristic it is of the written mode of language, the less it represents the relationship between mental processes and speech, which is its current justification.) After editing as necessary, the text has to be broken up into groups of words, and it is best if these are sense groups (usually a sequence of six to ten words, or a whole short sentence). The groups within sentences should not normally contain fewer than five words, otherwise the natural flow of speech may be distorted so that intonation becomes uncertain and unaccented vowels are given too much value. It is not helpful to the students' understanding to dictate one word at a time; in fact, this procedure destroys the point of the test.

There are various possibilities for administration of the test, relating to the number of complete and grouped readings and the amount of time allowed between groups. A good standard procedure is as follows (adapted from Alexander 1974: 155):

(Say) 'I'm going to read a text three times. The first time, just listen carefully. The second time, I shall read it more slowly and I shall pause frequently for you to write it down. The third time, I shall read it straight through again for you to check what you have written. Then you will have about two minutes at the end to read your work and correct it if you want to.

Now listen to it for the first time. Please do not write anything now. Just listen.'

(Now read the text straight through without making any of the pauses marked in it.)

'Now I'm going to read it more slowly and I shall pause often for you to write. I shall read each phrase ONCE only. Ready?'

(Now read the text again, each phrase once only, pausing where indicated (/) and judging when to read the next phrase by watching the majority of students as they write.)

'I'm going to read it for the last time. While I'm reading, check carefully what you have written; correct if necessary or add any words you may have missed. Ready?'

(Now read the text through without pausing and at the same speed as the first reading.)

(Give the students about two minutes to check what they have written.)

A text fitting the specification ('learning context') might start like this:

'The girls are all working/in small groups/of about four or five./The teacher is moving round the class/from group to group,/supplying bits of language/that the students need/and joining in the discussion./There is some Spanish being spoken,/but a lot of English phrases/are also being tried out/and when the teacher is present/the girls struggle hard/to communicate with her in English./There is also a good deal/of laughter and discussion./One girl in each group/ is writing down what the others tell her./'

The dictation should continue along the same lines for another hundred words or so, preferably with the groups of words becoming longer and the content more difficult (see page 27).

F: CONVERSATION

It was suggested earlier (page 5) that an individual conversation between a teacher and each student is an important element in the placement procedure. The difficulty is to find not only something useful to talk about but something which will at the same time allow a fair judgement to be made about the student's level. This requires some careful structuring of the content. A possible solution is to list at random some of the questions which need to be asked of a new student, and then choose the twenty-five which offer the best compromise between information to be obtained and language to be assessed. Finally, the questions should be arranged roughly in order of difficulty. This allows the teacher to choose which fifteen questions to ask as the test progresses, either taking them in order or omitting some and moving on to the more difficult ones, depending on the responses of the student. Such a list might be as follows:

1 Why are you learning English?
2 What do you like best in the English class?
3 What do you think about the tests?
4 Which was the easiest/hardest? Why?
5 What do you want to do/where do you want to go at the end of the course?
6 Have you read the handout/handbook/information sheet? Is there anything you don't understand? (Check an important point in it.)
7 Which options/classes have you chosen?
8 Have you filled in your timetable? (Check something in it.)
9 Which classroom will you be in? Do you know where it is? Tell me how you'll get there . . .

21 Do you need accommodation? What would you like/what have you got?
22 How far away is your home/your accommodation? How will you get here? How long will it take?

23 Have you met any of the students here before? Who? Where?
24 How did you hear about the school?
25 Is there anything you want to ask me about?

These questions are examples only, and obviously need to be drawn up to fit each school's circumstances, but they give an indication of the way in which the conversation can be organised so that it has some communicative value. There should also be a short introduction or greeting at the beginning before the marking of answers begins.

Alternatively, a more structured approach may be used, but as a result the conversation becomes more like an exercise undertaken for assessment purposes, rather than a real exchange of information. The starting point for this structural test could be a graded grammar such as Alexander *et al* 1975. If the top limit for material to be included in the test is Stage III (see specification), a logical procedure is to pick a series of suitable questions from the grammar at regular intervals through the first 104 pages of the book, which works out at one question from every four pages. However, it will not be possible to relate all these questions to the interview situation, and some supporting material will be needed. The simplest to find and use is probably a picture, in which case the specification of skills should be amended to read L2/*S2*/v.

The first few questions on a structured list of this kind might be as follows:

	Section in Alexander *et al* 1975
1 What's your name? (Spell it)	I.1.5
2 What's the colour of my pen/coat? And yours?	I.6.2
3 What can you see in this picture?	I.11.4
4 What has the man got in his hand? (What's in it?)	I.15.6
5 Why is he . . . ing?	I.20.3
6 Do you like wine/beer/ . . .? (What kind?)	I.24.1

7 What is the girl doing?   I.28.6
8 What's that thing on the table/wall . . .?   II.1.12
9 When do you think this party was?   II.3.5

Figure 11   F: conversation – picture

During the course of both these conversations, especially the second one since it is less realistic, the opportunity could be taken to introduce some kinds of classroom strategies such as provoking the student into asking for a repeat or a rewording by coughing in the middle of a sentence or phrasing a question in a more complex way than strictly necessary.

Since it consists of a series of individual statements, the conversation can best be marked on a communication-correctness basis, that is, one point is awarded to the student for making himself understood, and if this point is gained, but not otherwise, another point is awarded according to the accuracy of the language in which the answer is expressed. This system is explained in detail in Chapter 8.

5   Diagnostic tests

5.1   Review

The content of a diagnostic test is quite specific, referring back to recent classwork. It is intended to have positive results for the student by encouraging him with success or pointing out exactly what he needs to do to improve, and it should therefore be based on further examples of the kind of material which has been used in class. It should not be too difficult to establish the validity of the tests, since there is a direct link with known content, but reliability will need to be worked out on a basis other than well-spread distributions, because the intended pattern for the results is that the great majority of students should achieve high scores (perhaps 80 per cent or more). In general the tests should look like extensions of teaching material, so they should present few problems for teachers.

5.2   Commentary

A specification for a series of diagnostic tests is given in Figure 12. They do not form a battery like the placement tests because they are to be taken when needed, informally, and probably as part of a lesson. The teacher is likely to build up over a time a range of test material reflecting his teaching and the examples given here should be regarded only as starting points for extension and variation.

Figure 12   Diagnostic tests: a specification

Objectives (reference to objectives of unit just taught)
   Student can
1 (for example) recognise meanings of past tenses when he hears them in
   a context of 'everyday experiences'
2 (for example) use past tenses in context
3 . . .

Skills†

test G:	*L2*/v/t scripted speech
test H:	L2/*R2* scripted speech
test J:	R2/*W2*/e completion
test K:	*R2*/t completion
test L:	R2/*W2* transposition

Content
   language: (taken direct from course book and supplementary material)
             (for example) vocabulary of 'everyday experiences'; simple
             past; past perfect . . .
   subjects: (same as course book, and similar)
             (for example) travel: cars, public transport . . .

Formats
   test G: Listening text, 400 words + 15 items, m-c, 3 pictures
             (20–25 minutes)
   test H: listening text, 400 words, gaps chosen at about 20,
             20 items (20–25 minutes)
   test J: reading text, 250 words, gaps chosen at about 8, 30 items
             (20 minutes)
   test K: reading text, 200 words, gaps chosen at about 8, 25 items
             (15 minutes)
   test L: 10 sentences + guide words (20 minutes)

Rubrics as in classwork

Materials
   student: test sheets
   teacher: script or tape of scripted speech tests and playback
             equipment (language lab?); key sheets

Marking one point each item throughout (each test to be totalled
             separately; no composite score for all tests together)

---

† For key to coding of skills, see Figure 4, page 19.

The objectives given in Figure 12 are examples for tests *G* and *H: scripted speech* only. They refer to the content of the course unit from which they have been taken (*Mainline Progress B* [*MPB*] and *Access to English Open Road* [*AOR*], but should ideally be more precise than this. The skills do not include speaking because this is informally assessed continually during classwork and should not need separate testing for diagnostic purposes. If however the teacher thinks that the students would benefit from a diagnostic speaking test, one of those suggested for proficiency (Chapter 7) might be useful.

The specification for content is again rather sparse, like the objectives, and for much the same reason: it depends on how wide an area the teacher wants to assess and how long it is since the last test. For example, *G* or *H: scripted speech* could be given almost immediately after the content had been taught, but *J: completion* covers a longer time scale. The statements of content given in Figure 12 could be quite enough by themselves in some circumstances, but more material would usually need to be added.

The formats are more open-ended than for placement tests because the assessment is more informal and the results are to be used more casually. More particularly, tests *G* and *H: scripted speech* are suitable for use by the individual student on his own, either with a portable tape recorder or in a language laboratory, so that he can take as long as he needs to finish.

Another principle illustrated by *G: scripted speech* is the use of pictures from a textbook, which can either be the book used for the course or another. Using the course book has advantages since the pictures will be known to the students, and the meaning of certain conventional signs (such as arrows and question marks) will have been agreed. But it is helpful too in a more general way because familiar illustrations, for example the faces of the characters in the story line, will reduce the load of understanding, almost in the same way as a good rubric, allowing the student to concentrate his attention on the content rather than the mechanics of the test. The simplest way of using pictures for tests to be used within the school is photocopying. The copy can be labelled directly with identifying letters or numbers, or it can be cut up and used for multiple-choice picture tests (*G: scripted speech* is an example of this). In this case, photocopying is essential for the production of test sheets. An alternative is to copy or trace the illustrations by hand or, if the teacher can draw or obtain help from someone else who can, to produce new ones in the same style. (Useful guides to drawing pictures for language teaching [and therefore for testing] are Wright 1976 and Bowen 1982.)

Materials for diagnostic tests are usually treated like supplementary teaching materials; the sheets are issued to students and kept by them afterwards (but see contrary suggestion for test *G: scripted speech*). The normal procedure is to go through the tests with the class, using them for further teaching where this is suitable. There is usually no need to keep the answers confidential because there should not be any pressure on the results: there is no point in cheating in an informal test designed as a helpful check for the student. Recording the listening texts may not seem worthwhile if the tests are meant to be informal, but they will be much more flexible in use if this can be done. Also, test *H: scripted speech* requires gaps in the text, and this can be more easily and consistently arranged during a recording than in a live reading.

The marking is individual for each test. The interest of the results is not so much in the score as in the content to which the marks refer, so that there is no need to work out relative weights of scoring within a test or to achieve a balance between different tests. Total scores added up across several tests are irrelevant for diagnostic purposes.

5.3 Setting the tests

G: SCRIPTED SPEECH
As already mentioned, this test can be used either in class or for

self-assessment by a student working on his own. It is worked out by the test setter in the order: content – pictures – text. The first task is to find suitable pictures for representing whatever the content of the assessment is to be (in this example, events linked in past time) and then to write a text around the pictures which

Figure 13   Test G: scripted speech – test sheet

First of all, write the numbers 1–16 down the left side of a sheet of paper: this is your answer sheet. Then listen to the tape right through to the end without stopping. Go back to the beginning and start listening again. When you hear the signal, stop the tape and look at the first three pictures. One of them refers to something which happened before the time of the story. Write the letter for that picture, A, B or C, on your answer sheet. The answer to this first one is B. Now listen as far as the next signal and answer number 2. You can repeat parts of the tape as often as you like.

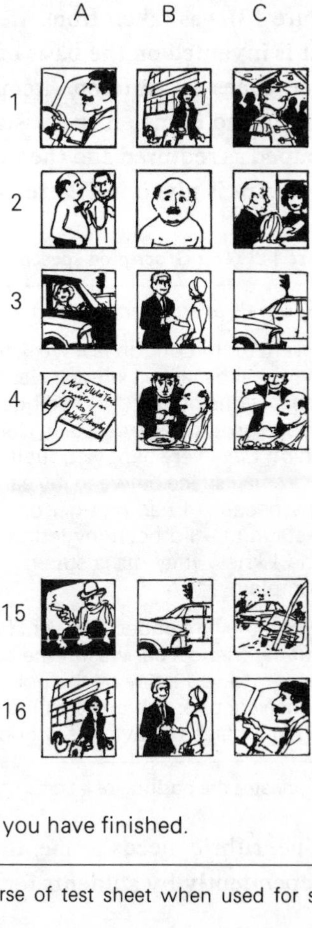

Please hand in this test sheet when you have finished.

(Keys: B C B A . . . C A; given on reverse of test sheet when used for self-assessment)

uses the necessary structures. An alternative for those who can draw is to find a suitable text and then invent pictures to illustrate it. There is small chance of finding compatible pictures and texts in different places (such as text book and cue cards, or magazine article and strip cartoon) but systematic collection of material over a period can produce some surprising and helpful coincidences.

The idea for the pictures used in the present example (see Figure 13) was taken from Alexander's *Mainline Progress B*. The text is invented on the basis of the pictures, using each one up to three times in different items. When the pictures have been allocated to items on the basis of the text, they are cut out and grouped as required and then stuck onto the test sheet. Part of the tapescript is given in Figure 14.

Figure 14   Test G: scripted speech – tapescript

George's evening in London

I went up to London last week to see a film with a new friend. I went in my car because I knew it was a long film and last time I had missed the last bus home. (*) I had booked the tickets in advance because I had to go and see a doctor in Harley Street before meeting my friend – I didn't feel very happy about it! (*) I watched my friend park her car in a small space between my car and a van marked 'Acme'. I was a bit shy because I had met her only once before. (*) We went into the restaurant – I'd been invited there the previous Saturday to a party and I knew they did a superb roast chicken, but this time I had to complain. (*) . . .

When the film ended we went back to the restaurant to get our cars, but my friend's car wasn't there. I knew what to do because I'd had my car towed away by the police once before. (*) I drove her to the police car park, which I'd found last time was next to the bus station. What a place to have to say goodbye! (*)

(*) indicates the position of a signal

The rubric needs some thought if the test is to be used independently by students for self-instruction (see side of Figure

13), but there is no need (as there was with *A: scripted speech*) to read the rubric onto the tape, since the student is under no pressure of time and can control repetitions to help him with the test system. For use in class, the test can be introduced orally by the teacher.

The recording does not include timed gaps, for the sound signal is enough to separate the sections, but the number of the item should be given after each signal. The signal itself need be no more than the sound of a pencil tapped on metal or glass (an ashtray or tumbler, for example). It is important that the text should be read at a natural speed, with shortened forms and other elisions, especially in this instance, where the student's understanding partly depends on the recognition of /d/ for 'had'.

The students should not write on the test sheets, but hand them in at the end of the test so that they can be used again. They would be of little use to a student in his own file, and are relatively expensive to produce. When the test is to be used for self-assessment it is helpful to give the keys on the back of the test sheet. If a transcript is issued to students it should be separate from the test sheet so that it can be used for class discussion and kept afterwards by the students. Also, as a separate sheet, it can be reproduced by less expensive methods than photocopying.

H: SCRIPTED SPEECH

This is a listening version of the completion test which can again (like *G: scripted speech*) be useful for self-assessment. The starting point here is an existing text from which the relevant verbs are taken out. The text is then recorded with a signal at each gap and the student writes the filler on a self-made answer sheet, as for *G: scripted speech*. Unlike the usual completion test, more than one word may be needed to fill a gap, and this should be explained to the student in the rubric and illustrated with an example.

A possible passage for assessing past tenses is given in Figure 15. The gaps need to be some way apart if the text is read at normal speed, as it should be, perhaps at every twenty words or so. The suggestions made for the rubric of *G: scripted speech* also apply here, but in this case the student may find the test sheets useful for further work and should be allowed to keep them if he wishes. The original ('exact') answers for the sample text are given in Figure 16, but any grammatically correct and plausible filler should be accepted: the form of the words is more important here than their content. This means that for self-assessment purposes a variety of acceptable answers should be given in the key, preferably those provided by experiments with native speakers.

Figure 15   Test H: scripted speech – text

I never cease to be fascinated by listening to old people reminiscing about what their bosses made them do when they were younger. I * to an old man the other day who was telling me about his boss forty-five years ago when he * work in the office of a firm in a small town in the west of England. He * me that his boss used to tell him off if he * him in church on a Sunday morning. But what amused me most was when he * the story about the way the boss used to inspect all his clerks to see if they * smartly enough for his liking. He used to walk into the office for no other reason than * at all his clerks' shoes to see if they were properly polished. He would make each man lift up his feet so that he could see whether the shoes * underneath – on the part between the sole and the heel. If anybody * to do this he would ask him to report to him the following day. He * a lecture to the blushing offender in front of the whole office . . .

(continued for a further eleven items to make a total of twenty, excluding the example)

Figure 16   Test H: scripted speech – key

1	(example) was talking	6	were dressed
2	started	7	to look
3	was telling	8	had been polished
4	didn't see	9	had neglected
5	told	10	would deliver . . .

(followed by a further eleven answers)

J: COMPLETION

Diagnostic tests sometimes refer further back than the previous lesson. This is the case with *J: completion*, which relates to two units in a course and to supplementary material (mainly vocabulary) introduced between elements in the units. This means that it involves sampling over a wider area than the previous two tests, and therefore has much in common with an achievement test.

Figure 17   Test J: completion

Fill in the gaps in this passage with ONE word each time.

A tall story
Let me tell you about my holiday last summer. I went to Athens and stayed at ..... hotel in the oldest part of ..... city. I must say I was ..... with the Acropolis, in fact I was ..... impressed I could hardly ..... to leave. But my ..... adventure was on ..... way home. In Athens I ..... bought a huge pullover ..... had put it in a ..... bag because there wasn't ..... room in my case. I took ..... on the aircraft with me because it ..... got my name on it and anyway I ..... something soft to wrap ..... the bottle of ouzo I was ..... back with me. I had also bought a ..... for taking corks out ..... bottles. I looked at my bag ..... all through the flight to make ..... the bottle was all right, . . .

(continued for a further ten items)

The difference between this test and a cloze test is that the gaps do not appear at regular intervals and that each gap is a deliberate choice related to past learning. In addition, the text was specially written and the words to be tested were worked in at approximately the right distance apart. It follows that the marking should be by the exact rather than by the acceptable method (see page 40), since the student has seen all the fillers before in other contexts. Ideally, however, marking is done alongside class discussion afterwards. One of the advantages of sampling more widely is that the content prompts the students to recall the context in which the original learning took place rather than just the individual structure or lexical item being tested. It becomes in effect a revision exercise with new variations based on the alternative fillers provided by the students. Working over the text in class like this is helped by not numbering the gaps as they would be in a more formal test: if the students want to talk about the items they have to produce phrases or sentences derived from the text rather than just refer to a number. A further method of exploitation is for the students to exchange test sheets for marking and work out a 'best' version in groups. Once again, each student's sheet at the end of the lesson, with his notes and variations, is a useful revision paper for his file.

Figure 18   Test J: completion – key

1	a	11	enough
2	the	12	it
3	impressed	13	hadn't
4	so	14	needed
5	bear	15	round
6	real	16	bringing
7	the	17	gadget
8	had	18	of
9	and	19	continually
10	carrier	20	sure . . .

(followed by a further ten answers)

K: COMPLETION

This is a multiple-choice version of the completion test format, offering the student alternatives for each gap. It is suitable only for testing vocabulary, or more accurately, the suitability of a word for a given context, since content words suggest more variations for fillers than function words (see *D: cloze*, page 40). If this kind of test is used for function words, grammatical absurdities cannot be avoided, and this is not compatible with the positive approach to learning which tests should encourage.

The best starting point for this test of vocabulary is to take a theme which has been covered recently in class and look for new material dealing with it, either in other course books or in a supplementary materials file. The theme in the example (Figure 19) is driving, so that the statement of objectives would read 'can understand the meaning of vocabulary associated with driving' and the content would consist of the words and phrases which were learnt in the relevant unit of the course. The test will probably have to sample this course content, partly because it will normally be too much to cover in a single test and partly because the parallel text which is to be used for the test will not cover exactly the same ground. The example presupposes that the twelve-page unit, 'A New Car' (*AOR*: 108–119), has been done. This unit contains three sections which include narrative, vocabulary linked to an illustration, dialogue, reading comprehension, group and pair work, writing, oral practice and listening comprehension. The parallel text was set for a listening comprehension exercise in another course (*MPB*: 127). The first step is for the test setter to underline in the texts, or list on a sheet of paper, those words which are relevant to the theme and which appear in both the parallel text and the course. In addition, it is helpful to indicate (perhaps with a wavy underlining) any other words which are associated with the theme and seem useful for the student to guess at in context. It may be necessary to omit several of these words eventually if there are too many for the student to attempt in the time available, but at this stage it is best to note them all and decide later which to leave out. The specification suggests twenty-five items in fifteen minutes, but this is a minimum and the teacher may well decide to extend the test if the parallel text he has found is long enough. It does not matter if the gaps occur quite close together in the text, since all of the items include the right answer and there is no need for the student to take into account the long-term meaning and structure of the passage, which he has to do in a cloze test. It is important, however, to look out for cases where the answer to one item depends on the answer to another. This is not necessarily to be avoided, but it should occur deliberately, not by accident.

Figure 19 Test K: completion – test sheet

	A	B	C	D
	travel	traffic	transit	travelling
	side	bonnet	back	wheel
	driving	reversing	running	moving
	side	boot	window	roof
	Highway Code	Police Act	Road Rules	Law of Traffic
	overhaul	go past	overtake	overlap
	dangerous	illegal	frightening	pointless
	roundabout	clearway	throughway	flyover
	drive	steer	twist	turn
	wait	park	unload	get in
	sign	signal	box	line
	road	traffic	T-junction	pedestrian

A: I watched a programme on television yesterday about . . 1 . . accidents. There was a policeman sitting at the . . 2 . . of a car. The car wasn't . . 3 . . . The policeman had his head out of the . . 4 . . and he spoke about the . . 5 . . .

B: What did he say?

A: The usual things. Don't . . 6 . . on a hill. It's . . 7 . . . Don't stop when you're on a . . 8 . . . Don't . . 9 . . right or left when it's forbidden. Don't . . 10 . . where there's a No Waiting. . . 11 . . . Don't accelerate when there's a . . 12 . . crossing ahead. Don't drive fast . . . .

(*Key:* B, D, D, C, A, C, A, B, B, A, D . . .)

Two or three alternatives are then thought out for each word or phrase (a thesaurus or dictionary of synonyms is helpful here). Four options (as used in the example) will make the test more reliable, but three is enough for relatively informal diagnostic purposes, and there is no point in making the task of setting the test more difficult than it need be. (The question of the number of options in multiple-choice tests is discussed in connection with O: *slanted text*.)

The rubric causes no problem for a student used to multiple-choice tests, and the materials are also simple: a duplicated sheet which the student may make notes on if the test is followed by class discussion, and which may be kept for future reference.

L: TRANSPOSITION

The final test to be suggested for diagnostic use is different from the others because it deals with language in sentences rather than in the larger context of a passage. This is to be avoided on the whole, because the larger the context, the more realistic the task for the student. If there is a need to set a diagnostic test of written production, however, it must be carefully controlled so that it can be specifically related to the previous teaching. The principle of the transposition test is well-known and frequently used in written work in class and outside it, and also in public examinations. The main advantage of this format is that, although it controls the student's response, it can be applied to a wide range of different constructions and is not particularly difficult to set. An instance, complete with rubric and example, is given in Figure 20. This particular test assesses the student's ability to handle changes in the form of a word, for example, 'lazy/laziness', 'try/trying', 'elected/election'. The format is obviously useful for the production of -ing forms and the derivation of abstract nouns.

Figure 20   Test L: transposition

Rewrite the sentences with the new beginnings. Do not change the meaning.

Example   The match was cancelled as it was raining.
Owing to . . .
Owing to rain, the match was cancelled.

a We enjoyed ourselves although we had no money.
In spite of . . .
b He failed the exam because he was so lazy.
Because of . . .
c Never buy shoes unless you try them on first.
Never buy shoes without . . .
d I am amazed that you don't know anything about the subject.
I am amazed at . . .
e We were late because we missed the train.
Through . . .
f Since he was elected, the Prime Minister has become very popular.
Since his . . .
g My wife has cleaned the house and cooked the dinner too.
As well as . . .
h As you failed your exam, you'll have to stay on at college for another year.
Because of . . .

Other examples are given by Heaton (1975: 35–39):

a I haven't written to you for a long time.
It's a long time . . . .
b In sunny weather I often go for a walk.
When the weather is sunny . . . .
c I was able to leave the office early yesterday.
It was possible . . . .
d Joe can sing better than you.
You cannot . . . .
e They believed that the earth was flat.
The earth . . . .

Each of these transpositions requires a different manipulation of structure, and sometimes a change of vocabulary as well, and models of other kinds are not difficult to find.

The distinction between transpositions as teaching/learning exercises and as diagnostic tests is that in the former case they are mainly used as a way of 'learning by doing', which often means doing it wrong and having it corrected. In tests, transpositions should be used to assess what has been taught, so that students should get them right most of the time and the few errors are helpful indications of points for revision. In addition, it seems that as exercises transpositions are listed almost at random, whereas for assessment the test setter should be using them for a particular purpose, grouping them into sets of the same kind and relating them directly to what has gone before.

The suggestion in the specification is that a set of ten transpositions is enough, but the teacher may regard this as a minimum for any one type of transposition, and wish to add more; or he may wish to include several groups of different transposition types in the same test.

6 Achievement tests

This chapter is concerned with achievement tests as they are designed and set by teachers for their own students, and not with public examinations such as the Cambridge and RSA certificates. It therefore follows the same pattern as the previous two chapters: a review of the conditions for school-based tests, an outline specification with comments on it and suggestions for suitable test formats and content.

6.1 Review

Designing and setting an achievement test is a bigger and more formal operation than the equivalent work for a diagnostic test, because the student's result is treated as a qualification which has a particular value in relation to the results of other students. An achievement test involves more detailed preparation and covers a wider range of material, of which only a sample can be assessed. The students will probably have been taught by more than one teacher over the previous year, and the best method of establishing an acceptable sample is by discussion and agreement among the teachers involved. Even if a teacher is working on his own, he will arrive at a better specification if he can discuss it with colleagues. The quality of the test is important for the results to be worthwhile, and if possible the test should be reviewed by several teachers at the various stages of the development process.

6.2 Commentary

The specification given in Figure 21 includes assessments of each of the four traditional skills, but courses in language for specific purposes (professional or technical) may concentrate on one or other of these skills and the tests relating to them should obviously do the same. There are three pairs of alternative test types, for listening, reading/writing, and speaking. The test battery is again a minimum and individual tests could be made longer or more tests added as required. In the latter case, the additional tests would improve the reliability of the battery as a whole and allow a wider variety of skills and content to be sampled.

Figure 21   Achievement tests: a specification

Objectives
　　Student can
1　(for example) understand conversation of general social interest . . .
2　(for example) understand spoken instructions . . .
3　. . .

Skills†
　　alternatives $\begin{cases}\text{test M:} & L2/\text{R2}/\text{t unscripted speech} \\ \text{test N:} & L2/\text{v/s/d unscripted speech}\end{cases}$
　　　　　　　　test O:　$R2$/t text and argument
　　alternatives $\begin{cases}\text{test P:} & \text{R2}/W2 \text{ letter} \\ \text{test Q:} & R2/W2 \text{ reorientation}\end{cases}$
　　alternatives $\begin{cases}\text{test R:} & \text{v}/S2 \text{ speak to pictures} \\ \text{test S:} & \text{c}/S2 \text{ talk}\end{cases}$

Content
　　language:　(for example) normal social chit-chat, as reflected in course/s; instructional language (numbers, measurement) . . .
　　subjects:　(for example) travel; human relations (weather, family, job); education; school procedures . . .

Formats
　　alternatives $\begin{cases}\text{test M:} & \text{listening text, 400 words + 20 items, m-c,} \\ & \text{3-option (25 minutes)} \\ \text{test N:} & \text{listening text, 800 words + 20 items, diagram (25} \\ & \text{minutes)}\end{cases}$

test O: reading text, 300 words + 20 items, m-c, 3-option (30 minutes)

alternatives {
test P: short stimulus, write 5 points (20 minutes)
test Q: reading text, 150 words, write 10 points (30 minutes)
}

alternatives {
test R: 2 pictures, discuss (3 minutes)
test S: prepared talk on topic (3 minutes)
}

total test time: 75 or 80 minutes + 3 minutes each student (test R or test S)

Rubrics practised in advance; examples essential

Materials
  student: test booklet, answer sheet
  teacher: tape of unscripted speech and playback equipment; pictures for speaking; topics for talk; key sheet and marking schemes; scoring sheets for speaking

Marking
  alternatives {
  test M: 30 marks (30 items × 1)
  test N: 30 marks (30 items × 1)
  }
  test O: 20 marks (20 items × 1)
  alternatives {
  test P: 20 marks (5 points × 4)
  test Q: 20 marks (10 points × 2)
  }
  alternatives {
  test R: 30 marks (5 categories × 6)
  test S: 30 marks (5 categories × 6)
  }
  (total marks: 100)

† For key to coding of skills, see Figure 4, page 19.

As before, both objectives and content are specific to the circumstances in which the tests are to be used, so that the statements in the sample specification are only a beginning. Suitable difficulty levels for different groups of students can be arrived at by varying the requirements of the test in relation to the same text. For example, lower level students may be expected to show only general or gist understanding, but more advanced students may be asked to interpret more subtle aspects of the communication, such as the intentions of speakers and the relationships between them. If the teacher is compelled to simplify the text, it is better to delete the difficult parts and leave

given once complete at the beginning, and then repeated in overlapping sections, but does not have a final complete reading. On the other hand, *N: unscripted speech* is heard only once (see page 73). Other factors concerning the difficulty of the text are of course the density of the thought expressed in it and the speed at which it is spoken. These two tend to influence a text in inverse ratio: the more difficult the content, the more slowly it is spoken. When unscripted speech is recorded for the test it is important that there should be no attempt to read it word for word. The transcript (Figure 22) includes some (but not all) of the original hesitations, false starts, repetitions and so on, but they are there only as a guide to where the flow of thought is broken, and the 'readers' should make approximately equivalent breaks and changes of direction in their own way. This may seem a lot to ask, but it is surprising what a few minutes' practice can do to make the conversation sound unrehearsed!

Figure 22　M: unscripted speech – tapescript

> *Announcer* (A): Test 2. Listen to this conversation. You will hear it right through to the end once and then you will hear it again in sections, with pauses which will give you time to answer.
>
> *Woman's voice* (B): . . . and I flew when I went to Italy when I left school when I was seventeen and hated it really hated it.
>
> *Man's voice* (C): oh I love flying
>
> B:　and I swore then that I would never do it again
>
> C:　how funny
>
> B:　if I could possibly manage it
>
> C:　oh I enjoy flying very much I mean this sort of feeling of being pushed up into the sky sort of taking off at tremendous pace and shooting up
>
> B:　no I I'd have hysterics
>
> C:　oh dear
>
> B:　I think it's also
>
> C:　so you go by sea and and boat and train and things
>
> B:　yes yes it's like claustrophobia too, sort of being shut away
>
> C:　yes . . . not like that at all
>
> B:　doesn't affect me in a boat which of course is much the same
>
> C:　and the underground?

B: don't like the underground
C: don't like the underground
B: though I use it yes I I make myself go on it but I'm never very happy I sit there and
C: it's quite frightening actually
B: and if it stops in a tunnel
C: if it stops that's right
B: I'll sit there and twiddle my fingers and and
C: yes (laughter) oh well yes I was sitting in one that had got stuck and it was about the time when there were those bomb scares (yes) and people were getting quite edgy (yes) . . .

(continued up to a total of approximately 400 words)

A: That is the end of the conversation. Now look at the items in your test booklet.
PAUSE 10 SECONDS
A: For each item there is only one answer. Put a circle round A, B or C on your answer sheet to indicate which you think is best for each item. Here is an example.
B: . . . and I flew when I went to Italy when I left school when I was seventeen and hated it really hated it
C: oh I love flying
B: and I swore then that I would never do it again
C: how funny
B: if I could possibly manage it
C: oh I enjoy flying very much I mean this sort of feeling of being pushed up into the sky sort of taking off at tremendous pace and shooting up
B: no I I'd have hysterics
A: Now read the example.
PAUSE 10 SECONDS
A: The answer is B. Now listen to the first section.
C: oh I enjoy flying very much I mean this sort of feeling of being pushed up into the sky sort of taking off at tremendous pace and shooting up
B: no I I'd have hysterics
C: oh dear
B: I think it's also
C: so you go by sea and and boat and train and things
B: yes yes it's like claustrophobia too, sort of being shut away
C: yes . . . not like that at all
B: doesn't affect me in a boat which of course is much the same
C: and the underground?
B: don't like the underground

```
C:   don't like the underground
B:   though I use it yes I I make myself go on it but I'm never very
     happy
A:   One: A, B or C?
     PAUSE 10 SECONDS
A:   Now listen to the next section. . . .
```

(Four items are given in Figure 23)

One small point, which seems trivial but is very helpful to both students and item writers, is to ensure that the speakers name each other near the beginning of a conversation. This is not so important if they are easily distinguishable (for example, a man and a woman), but the owners of voices are easily confused, even if the voices themselves are contrasted. The item writer too can identify the speakers more easily and economically ('David' rather than 'the man who . . .').

Items

Writing multiple-choice items relating to listening texts clearly has much in common with writing them for reading texts, and since the relationship is more demanding in the latter case, the whole area of technique is discussed later on (see *O: text and argument*, page 76ff.). The differences to note here are that, as with true/false items, there can be considerable variety in the demands that multiple-choice items make on the student's understanding of the text, although these demands must obviously relate to an aural rather than visual dimension. This is not only a matter of memory span and the sounds of words (rather than their shape and organisation on the page) but also a matter of purpose: what spoken language is used for and how this differs from what written language is used for. This variety of purpose becomes clear when the text is considered as a communication, which is the basis of the following discussion.

Two varieties of unscripted speech are represented here: general conversation (test *M*) and a talk (test *N*, page 73ff). The items for the first of these should explore the relationship between the speakers, the reasons for hesitations and repetitions, the attitudes of the speakers to the subject they are talking about, and, of course, the subject itself. The talk for test N consists of factual instructions given by one speaker, so the content of the items is different (see the next section). But both these sets of items will be different from those for reading. They take a longer span of text as a basis, partly because the aim of listening is not to pick up incidental detail (if a point is important it will be emphasised by the speakers), but mainly because spoken text repeats content as well as individual words in ways which are not acceptable in print. For example, in Figure 22, B's first four statements ('really hated it' . . . 'never do it again' . . . 'possibly manage it' . . . 'have hysterics') are all elaborations of the same idea, and her sixth statement ('claustrophobia') picks it up again. This means that items can be written to find out whether the student has understood the strength of the speaker's feeling (which would probably be represented in writing by one strongly worded phrase); the difference of C's view from B's (in written form probably preceded by some direct expression of contrast like 'however', 'but', 'on the other hand'); and C's sympathy, as expressed in the suggestion 'sea and boat and train' (in writing, more likely to be directly stated in 'I'm sorry to hear . . .', 'What a pity you don't . . .').

The items in Figure 23, relating to the emotional content of the conversation, should of course be only part of the test, and other items should be written about the factual content. Even here, however, there is a difference between listening and reading, and the items should take into account unclear statements, false starts, contradictions and so on, in finding out whether the student has understood what the speaker means (sometimes in contrast to what he says).

It was stated earlier in connection with *A: scripted speech* that there are dangers in writing true/false items on the text as read in a

Figure 23   M: unscripted speech — items

1   What does the woman feel about flying?
    A   She doesn't like it much
    B   She is uncertain about it
    C   She will not do it

2   What is the man's view of flying?
    A   He thinks the woman is right
    B   He would rather go by sea
    C   He is excited by it

3   How does the man react to the woman's view about flying?
    A   He thinks it is silly
    B   He takes no notice of it
    C   He tries to understand it

4   They both say 'don't like the underground'. This means
    A   he doesn't like it
    B   she doesn't like it
    C   neither of them likes it

transcript rather than as heard on a tape (page 34). This is still true for multiple-choice items, but the task of writing them is so much more exacting that reference has to be made to a transcript to ensure that all the content of the items is plausible. For the same reason, a transcript is important at the review stage, because listening to the tape repeatedly for confirmation takes too long. But this makes it all the more important that checks are made to ensure that the items really do assess understanding by listening.

N: UNSCRIPTED SPEECH

Much of the above discussion also applies to this test. The principles behind it are that the information presented in informal speech usually contains grains of important fact in large amounts of chaff; that understanding involves sifting the one from the other; and that the student can show his understanding without having to tackle true/false or multiple-choice items, or produce a lengthy written or spoken answer. In this test he uses simple labels (single words, letters or figures).

This example of the test consists of a talk given by a teacher on the coming week's activities, which vary for three different groups of students. He speaks informally, from a copy of the timetable with all three alternatives written on it. He should not speak from a script. The talk is given once only, but with plenty of repetition within it. For an achievement test, the text must be recorded, so that students at different sittings of the test all hear exactly the same version (a question of reliability). If the same kind of test is used for diagnostic purposes or (informally) for proficiency, the teacher can give the talk live.

Before handing out the test sheets (the timetable in Figure 25) the teacher writes A, B or C in the space marked 'Group', arranging it so that about a third of the class is in each group. He can incidentally make cheating more difficult by giving sheets for different groups to neighbouring students. Each student listens for those parts of the talk which are relevant to him. Some of the elements (for example, meals on the Saturday) are common to all groups, and some choices for individuals can be included too. The marking is simple: three different overlays are prepared, one for each group's answers. The test sheets are then sorted into the three groups, each of which is marked in turn.

Figure 24   Test N: unscripted speech – tape transcript

(Listen to this talk about the programme for the week. Write on your timetable the things you need to know.)

Good morning. Now I hope you've all got your timetables. You'll see that there are quite a lot of gaps on it and I'm going to tell you about the programme. Fill in the spaces. Now what you're doing at any given point in the day depends on the group you're in, and you'll see that at the top of your timetable it says Group A or B or C, depending on which group you're in, so if you've got Group A at the top you listen for what Group A is doing, and so on for Group B and Group C.

Now the first thing is the morning programme. Groups A and B do communication and writing at 9.30 and 10.45 on Monday, Wednesday and Friday, so could you write in on your timetable, if you are in Groups A and B, communication 9.30, writing at 10.45, for Monday, Wednesday and Friday. All right? And if you're in Group C, at the same times, Monday, Wednesday and Friday, it's 9.30 for writing and 10.45 for communication. All right?

Now on Tuesdays and Thursdays it's again alternate. On Tuesdays and Thursdays Groups A and B do writing at 9.30 and communication at 10.45, and Group C does communication at 9.30 and writing at 10.45, so fill in those as well.

Now on Tuesday, Wednesday and Thursday afternoons you will see that you have time free, yes? . . .

Figure 25   Test N: unscripted speech – test sheet

Group   TIMETABLE

	Monday	Tuesday	Wednesday	Thursday	Friday	Saturday
8.00	BREAKFAST					
9.30						
10.20	COFFEE					
10.45						
12.15	LUNCH					
2.00 2.50	Intro Work- shop	Free	Free	Free	Intro Work- shop	
4.00	TEA					
6.00	SUPPER					
8.00			pub visit		party	SUPPER

Other examples of this test type are given in Heaton (1975: 65ff). Most of these are more like exercises in comprehension than representations of possible language uses.

O: TEXT AND ARGUMENT

Principles

This is a 'reading comprehension' test with multiple-choice items, but it requires understanding of the author's intentions as well as of the factual content of the text. It is labelled 'text and argument' because all texts are written from a particular point of view and the test should include some assessment of the implications of this for the reader. As with the tests of listening just discussed, many different assessments are possible within the format of reading text and items, but only a few examples of the most useful ones can be analysed here.

Text

The text for this type of test should contain factual information, logical progression of argument, and bias originating from the author's view of his subject. A magazine feature by an astrologer, for example, might seem to be a good text because it deals with everyday events and their effect on the individual, and is written in such a way as to involve the reader in the events described. The requirements of an astrologer's statements, however, mean that there must be general reference to possible happenings which can be interpreted in different ways according to the reader's situation. The reader supplies at least half the meaning by finding events in his own life to which the astrologer's predictions could apply. There is not enough factual meaning, little variety in construction and a non-committal style which deliberately avoids any personal involvement of the writer.

The passage for this test (Figure 26) is taken from a newspaper article. It was chosen because its subject is of general interest and its language content suitable for students at an intermediate level. It is concerned with a common problem, that of young people moving forward into the world of adults and learning how to cope with it and yet at the same time reacting against training. The text itself is a combination of fact and opinion which will give plenty of material for items, and it is written with commitment: a good example of a 'text and argument'.

Figure 26   Test O: text and argument – passage

Few would argue with the need to train car drivers before letting them loose on the highway. Yet a 16-year-old can buy a 50cc moped and a 17-year-old can buy a 250cc motorbike with a top speed in excess of 100 mph without being required to pass even the most cursory of tests. Last year only 12,000 of the 250,000 new riders to take to the road enrolled in the National Motor Cycle Training Scheme, an operation funded by the industry in an attempt to cut the appalling accident statistics. The scheme has facilities for 240,000 new riders, has 403 centres and 1,475 qualified instructors. Why is it failing? The answer may lie in the word instructor. That, certainly, is the answer Dennis Tanner would give you. Dennis became a household motorcycling name as the wheelie king. Now 37, and married with three sons all of whom ride bikes, his vocation is to make motorcycling safe without losing any of its excitement . . .

(the next seventy words have been omitted)

. . . those young riders in whom Dennis Tanner is particularly interested. These are the teenagers, mostly boys, who see the motorbike as a symbol of independence, maturity and frequently rebellion. These are the kids who are soon to leave school or who have just left. They've had enough of being taught. They want action and many of them will die pursuing it.

Items

The five items given in Figure 27 are intended to assess different aspects of reading comprehension. Item 1 is concerned with the meaning of a single word; Item 2, the meaning of a phrase; Item 3, the meaning and implication of the author's use of a particular word; Item 4, the author's view of the situation described; Item 20, the structure and reference of part of the passage. ('Author' is used here to avoid confusion with 'test writer' or 'item writer'. On the test paper, however, the word 'writer' is to be preferred: see Items 3 and 4.)

Figure 27 Test O: text and argument – items

1 '. . . to *train* car drivers . . .' means
   A to help them
   B to test them
   C to instruct them
   D to tell them

2 What does a 16-year-old have to do before he can ride a motorcycle on the road?
   A Pass a short driving test
   B Pass the same test as a car driver
   C Take a training course
   D Take no test or training at all

3 What is the writer's view about accidents?
   A They occur far too frequently
   B They are more likely with powerful motorcycles
   C They result from the lack of training schemes
   D They often involve young riders

4 According to the writer, what is the matter with the training scheme?
   A Not enough courses are provided
   B The courses sound too much like school
   C The motorcycle industry does not take enough interest
   D There are too many new riders . . .

(the next fifteen items have been omitted)

20 Which of these is most likely to follow after the end of the passage?
   A But show them a way of finding action . . .
   B Against considerable odds, Dennis Tanner has proved . . .
   C 'Safe riding is 50 per cent machine control . . .'
   D It was established 18 months ago, not far from . . .

At this point some technical terms need to be explained. The word 'item' is used rather than 'question' because, as in the case of the first example in Figure 27, its form is often a statement rather than a question. The first part of the item is the *stem* (see Figure 28): it sets the problem that the candidate has to solve and should help him towards the answer. For example, if the stem in Figure 28 were merely 'This passage', the candidate would have to read the rest of the item right through before he found out what he was being asked to understand. The alternatives between which he has to choose are the *options*; the right one is the *key* and the wrong ones are the *distractors*.

Figure 28   The multiple-choice item: technical terms

```
STEM     —  This passage comes from an article about
OPTIONS  —  A   car drivers           (DISTRACTOR)
         —  B   driving tests         (DISTRACTOR)
         —  C   young motorcyclists   (KEY)
         —  D   racing motorbikes     (DISTRACTOR)
```

The number of options in the item is affected by the type of test in which it occurs and the level of reliability required of the test as a whole. There are usually either three, four or five. In a listening test it is important that the items should demand as little effort of understanding as possible from the student, because the intention is to assess his understanding of what he hears (the passage), not of what he reads on his test sheet (the items). (Some tests of listening attempt to make the content more consistent by recording the items on the tape, so that the whole of the test material is heard, but this causes more problems than it solves for teachers setting their own tests.) The understanding assessed by a test of reading, on the other hand, is sometimes considered to begin with the first word of the passage and finish with the last word of the last item. In a listening test, therefore, there should be as few options as possible and in a reading test as many as are necessary to achieve an acceptable level of reliability. The problem here is guessing: if the student guesses at random through a multiple-choice test in which there are three options for each item, he could get a third of them right by chance, but if there are five options random answering is likely to give him only a fifth of the total score. The theory, therefore, is that the more options there are the better, though setting items with more than five is impractical. For reasons of validity, however, and also depending on the use of results, three-option items may be preferred. In this case, there are two ways of reducing unreliability. One way is to lengthen the tests, and the other is to apply a statistical correction for guessing (see glossary).

Writing items

Several basic principles can be illustrated by reference to Item 1 (Figure 27). Firstly, it is helpful to the student if there is some kind of rhythm in the options, and this is usually achieved by parallelism. One of the classic rules for item writing is that there should be a minimum of repetition, which in this case would suggest that the 'to' in each option should be taken back up to the end of the stem. There are two reasons for breaking this rule here: the fact that the syntax of the sentence links the word to the following verb, not to 'means'; and the need to make each option as far as possible a unit of meaning.

A second basic principle is that the point at issue, especially if it involves a quotation from the passage, should be clearly indicated for the student. In Item 1, quotation marks, italics and continuation marks have been used, but in a long passage line references are also helpful.

Thirdly, the item illustrates the rule that options should be plausible, not just a random set of errors. It makes the student compare the word 'train' with four others, which all fit grammatically into the same phrase as it stands, and which would all fit semantically into the same phrase if it were used in other contexts. There is no reference to other meanings of 'train' (series of carriages drawn by an engine or lengthened skirt of a dress), since there is nothing in the passage which suggests links with these other meanings. There are no errors either, for example, in spelling or grammatical form, because the objective is to assess understanding of the text, not recognition of error.

Item 2 assesses understanding of a phrase: 'without being required to pass even the most cursory of tests'. This is a wider ranging item than the first one because if the candidate is unsure of the meaning of the phrase concerned, there are clues elsewhere in the passage which will guide him ('train car drivers', 'yet', 'only 12,000 of the 250,000', 'accident', 'instructors' and so on). The understanding needs to be structural ('without being', 'even the most . . . of') as well as semantic ('required', 'pass', 'cursory'), and it is likely that if he does not know at once what the meaning of the whole phrase is, the candidate will use his partial knowledge of elements within it, and his understanding of the item's relationship with other parts of the text, to arrive at an answer.

As with Item 1, all the distractors are plausible within the structure and meaning of the item, and this time they also relate to specific points appearing in the passage, either directly or by implication. However, there is a classic rule that a single negative option will tend to attract candidates because it is unique, whether or not it is the key, and should therefore be avoided. The reason for breaking the rule in this case is that the option describes another logical possibility which happens to be right: it is no more negative in the context of this item than the common formula 'none of these'. Nevertheless, as a general rule, none of the options should stand out from the others in any way, grammatical or otherwise.

It is important that all the options should have some plausible connection with the content of the passage. Sometimes, however, this can result in the use of direct quotations from the text for the distractors and a paraphrase for the key; or, less commonly, a direct quotation for the key, and paraphrases for the distractors. For example, Item 2 could read:

> What does a 16-year-old have to do before he can ride a motorcycle on the road?
> A   Buy a 250cc motorbike
> B   Train like car drivers
> C   Enrol in the National Motorcycle Training Scheme
> D   Take no test or training at all

Here, the three virtually direct quotations from the passage make the one paraphrase sound like an invention for testing purposes and therefore the right answer, which it is.

Item 3 assesses understanding of the meaning and implication of a word used in a particular context, in this case the author's personal view of the situation. The stem follows a common formula which is helpfully non-committal: 'What does the writer feel about. . . .? The use of 'about' avoids prejudgements on the test writer's part which make it difficult to find reasonable distractors. If the stem had been 'The writer says that accidents are', the item is already restricted to what actually appears in the passage and cannot take into account either the implications of what is written there or the author's views on his subject.

It is often helpful to write a first attempt at a stem and then produce at random as many options as possible within a few minutes: keys, distractors, absurdities, possibilities, good ideas and bad ones, one after another. This rapid generation of ideas seems to gather momentum as it goes on, and it is often possible to produce as many as twenty-five options within three or four minutes. All except the number required by the test (three or four) will of course be discarded, but in the process the original idea may be shown to need major recasting and ideas for new items will often appear. The collection of options will give a good indication of what the stem should be aiming at and, after some refining, two or even three items may be written as a result of the brief initial brainstorming. The alternative is often a long period of thought over a single item, which began with a bad idea for a stem and which may never reach a wording in which it can be used. The draft options for Item 3 are given in Figure 29.

The subject of Item 4 is one of the author's conclusions about the situation described, an interpretation of the facts. The importance of logic in the items as well as in the passage is illustrated by the first draft of the stem for this item, which read: 'Why does the writer think so few motorcyclists enrolled for a

Figure 29   Test O: text and argument – draft of Item 3

What does
~~is~~   say   the number of
the writer's ~~thinks~~ ~~view~~ about/ m/c accidents ?

            there are
            they are inevitable
            they are far too numerous
            they can be reduced
            they cannot be reduced
            they are horrifying
            they result from a lack of training
            they happen mainly with new riders
            they are the result of inexperience
            they are the fault of the industry
            the m/c industry does nothing about them
            nobody cares about them but him
            nobody cares enough about them
            the training scheme would reduce them
            they would be reduced if there were more
                                instructors

            industry is trying to do something about them

            the training scheme does | no good
                                    | not help

---

                              frequently
Say | They ~~are~~ occur far too ~~many of them~~
write | about   likely
think/   more / ~~frequent~~ with powerful motorcycles
           They are ~~inevitably~~ caused by ~~high~~ speeds
                                fast ~~driving~~
                                   riding

          unaffected
        are not ~~reduced~~ by the
    They ~~result from lack of~~ training schemes
    – – – – – – – – –

        y   often involve   young
    There ~~are more of them with new~~ riders

training course last year?' The answer was intended to be derived from the last two sentences of the passage, but it could equally well have been 'Because the statistics say so'. In the first draft, too, option C read: 'The motorcycle industry takes no interest in them'. But 'them' could refer either to 'training courses' or to 'motorcyclists', an ambiguity which could not be allowed to stand as a distractor (it is just as wrong in either case). The important point here is that the candidate's understanding must be assessed by the relevance and consistency of the items in relation to the passage, not by ambiguities within the items.

One of the most helpful principles for item writers is: 'Distractors may be relevant but untrue, or true but irrelevant: only keys are both relevant and true'. Options A and C are relevant to the passage but not a true interpretation of it; and D is factually true according to the passage but not relevant to the stem. As in the first item, a rhythm is achieved by parallelism in the options, with a negative followed by 'enough' in A and C, and 'too much' and 'too many' in B and D.

Item 20 is concerned with the structure of the passage. It requires the candidate to appreciate connections and references in the build-up of the argument. All the options come from the same article from which the passage is taken (and therefore belong to the same author), and yet only one of them could follow at this point in the argument.

There is a very wide scope for the assessment of understanding by multiple-choice items, and a very large number of examples can be found in books on language testing such as Heaton (1975), Harris (1969), and Valette (1977), who gives examples in French, German and Spanish. The relationship between the text and the items is explored in depth by Widdowson (1978).

P: LETTER

The most likely reason for students needing to write in real life is the letter, which in the context of this test could mean anything

Figure 30   P: letter – stimulus

You have 20 minutes for this test.
Read the following advertisement.

Stay with a family

Learn the language, get to know the British people, or just have a holiday.
Any age from 12 years, any part of the country, any time of the year. Also
group visits and guided tours.
Write to Mr David Brooks, Contact Ltd., Raven Hall Road, Northings,
Fordash FD26 1HF.

You want to have a holiday in Britain. Write a letter to Mr Brooks. In your
letter tell him:
1   Where you want to go in Britain
2   What rooms you need
3   The dates of your stay
and ask about:
4   prices
5   places to visit
Write your letter on the next page. Put the date at the top.

---

from a holiday postcard to a business contract. The problem is not
so much in setting it as in marking it (see Chapter 8), but there are
several important aspects of setting which will make the marking
easier. The stimulus should be as short and clear as possible, but at
the same time it must give an adequate framework for the
student's writing. Pictures or other visual material can be used as
a stimulus (for example writing to describe something that is for
sale), but then there can be difficulties of interpretation.

It is particularly important for the student to know who he is
writing to and for him to be aware that this will affect what he
writes. For example, the stimulus given in Figure 30 asks the
student to write to a man in England whose business it is to
understand the English of non-native speakers. In this case it
should be obvious that sense is considerably more important than
form.

If, however, it was a letter to the Gas Board or to a Tax
Inspector, it would obviously need to be more formally and

accurately worded. A decision has to be made by the setter of the test about the attitude to be taken to letter conventions. These range from the correct order of the date (4/11/82 is ambiguous, for example, where both American English and British English speakers are involved) to matching 'Dear Sir' with 'Yours faithfully' and 'Dear Mr Smith' with 'Yours sincerely'. They may be ignored or given some weight in the marking, but the student must know what is expected.

It is better for the student not to be asked to count words, but to make a series of points (five in this test). The assessment then takes account of how well the message has been transmitted, which includes how much language has been needed to express it.

Q: REORIENTATION

This test takes the principle of transposition and sets it in the context of appropriateness. The student is given a passage to read, which is usually a narrative or the discussion of an issue (political or social); the essential ingredient is that there are at least two viewpoints. The task is to transform the content of the passage into another form as the result of a change of viewpoint. The simplest case is a straightforward change from direct to indirect speech, such as that given in Figure 31. Even here there is some change of formality ('You can't take prams in there' has to be reworded in the passive, using 'allowed' or another official-sounding verb). More complex reorientations can be required if the text is a narrative involving three or more people in a series of events. Rewriting these events from the point of view of one of the characters, for example in a diary, or recalling them at home to the family, or writing a letter about them, should reveal the relationships between the people involved and the different emphasis put on the same events by various participants. The main problem with this test is to control the material which the student should include in the new account of events, so that one student's version can be fairly compared with another's. One solution to this is to italicise key words in the text as an indication of the topics which are to be included (see Figure 32). The marking (see Chapter 8) is based on these topics and gives credit for grammatical, semantic and attitudinal content. The rubric is rather complicated, and the test should not be used without practice in class beforehand.

Figure 31   Q: reorientation – text 1

A newspaper reporter is interviewing a young mother after her baby has been stolen.

REPORTER: Could you tell me exactly when and how it happened Mrs Stone?

MRS STONE: Yes, I can remember it very clearly. It was on Monday morning. I was doing some shopping in the supermarket, the one in Tottenham High Street, you know. You can't take prams in there so I left the baby in the pram outside. I wasn't going to be long. I had only a few things to buy, you see. Well, when I came out, the pram was there but little Jeremy had disappeared. I asked a few people standing around but they hadn't noticed anything. So then I called the police. That was two days ago. I can't think why they wanted to steal him.

REPORTER: Thank you, Mrs Stone. And, don't worry. I'm sure the police are doing everything they can to help find your son.

Imagine you are a newspaper reporter and you are going to write an article in the local newspaper about the baby-snatching. Try to report only the important facts in the right order. Start like this:

BABY-SNATCHING OUTSIDE SUPERMARKET

A young baby was stolen on Monday morning outside the supermarket in Tottenham High Street. When asked how it had happened, Mrs Stone, the mother of the baby, said that she was . . . .

Figure 32   Q: reorientation – text 2

Read the passage below.
He walked over to his office and went straight to the telephone.
'Can I *speak* to Mr Ward?' he asked.
'He isn't *in*,' a woman's voice told him.

'Who's that? Is *Miss* Ward in?'

'It's me, sir, Blodwen. I'm cleaning the house. Miss Ward *isn't* in, either.'

'*Where* are they, Blodwen?' He knew Blodwen Jones. She was a nice girl but her mind worked *slowly*.

'In *London*, sir – I think.'

'When will they be *back*?'

'I don't *know*, sir. They said that they would telephone me.'

'I see. Thank you, Blodwen.' He put the telephone down. Then he picked it up again and asked for a *London* number. When someone answered, he asked, 'Can I speak to Mr *Thurston*, please?'

'Who is that?'

'It's David Morgan here, *Mrs* Thurston.' He had recognised her *voice* . . .

Now write two different versions of the story.

1 Write the note that Blodwen left for Mr Ward before she went home. Start like this:

   Mr Morgan rang. He asked if he could speak to you, but I said you weren't in . . .

2 Write what David Morgan reported to the police later. Start like this:

   I telephoned Mr Ward but he was out. I asked if Miss Ward was there, but Miss Jones said she was not in either . . .

You can get marks in four ways: writing something about each of the words which are italicised in the passage; using grammar accurately; using words which are not in the passage but help to explain the story; writing like the person you represent (in this case, Blodwen and David Morgan).

R: SPEAK TO PICTURES

The use of pictures in speaking tests is common, but the assessment is often only vaguely controlled. Telling the story of a sequence of four pictures or describing what can be seen in one picture usually produces limited forms of language: some vocabulary and a series of verbs in the same tense. A more structured test can be arranged with the help of two pictures, which differ from each other in various ways. An example is given in Figure 33. The procedure is that the teacher and student have one picture each and without showing it to the other, they find out what the differences are. The fact that the teacher knows what is in both pictures (at least in general terms) is a disadvantage which can be overcome by having students take the test in pairs, with the teacher observing and assessing. Pairs of pictures with more

Figure 33   R: speak to pictures – stimulus

subtle differences are regularly published in newspapers and magazines, and provided the vocabulary required is not too demanding, these can be used as a basis for tests. Single cartoons or series of pictures may be used in similar ways as material for structured discussion (Revell 1979: 67, Heaton 1975: 93).

S: TALK ON TOPIC

Students are not often encouraged to prepare their own material for a test, but for a student to speak for a few minutes on a topic which he has chosen and about which he has something to say requires considerable organisation of thought and of the language to match it. The most liberal version of this test is to allow the student to choose his own subject and prepare as much as he likes. The only limits imposed are that he must not produce a memorised speech and that he must stop within the time allowed. The assessment can take into account presentation, use of visual aids (if any) and audience contact, as well as the use of language (Burniston 1968: 22). A restricted version is for the teacher to give the student three topics a few minutes before the test, and then in the test the teacher asks which one the student would like to talk about, or chooses one himself and tells the student to talk about it. In this case, the assessment is concerned much more with language than with content, and the student cannot be expected to express any great commitment to the subject. Between these two extremes there is the possibility of the student choosing, say, five topics in which he is interested, and the teacher asks him to talk about one or two of these, again within a strict time limit. In principle, the student should be encouraged to use the language for his own purposes in tests, as well as inside and outside the classroom.

7 Proficiency tests

7.1 Review

The two main characteristics of proficiency tests, according to the description in Chapter 1, are that they relate to the applications of what has been learnt, and that they have to be based on a specification of the language that is going to be needed in these applications. An assessment of proficiency can be helpful in a variety of circumstances. It can be a formal test to decide whether a student is likely to cope with a course of specialist study (for example, a postgraduate course at a university or a professional training course for a technician), or it can be useful as an informal check on how well the student can put into practice the language he has been learning. There are elements of proficiency in several kinds of test, including placement, diagnostic and achievement.

The analysis of students' language needs can be a very complex process, but even when the course content has been defined along these lines, the test specification has to be drawn up, as always, within the limits set by reliability, validity and practicality. The ideal test might be to send the student out with a tape recorder in a place where the language is spoken to see how he copes with language in real life. If he finds his way to the bank, cashes a cheque, buys the right size of shirt and is a social success at a party (for example), the only task for the test assessor is to listen to the tape to see how effectively the student did all these things. But the test has to be more controlled than this if the results are to have any value for the student. Real life is too random, and a structure has to be set up which will allow a comprehensible interpretation to be made of the results of the assessments.

There are two kinds of assessment which will set up a structure of this kind: for present purposes they will be called 'representative' testing, which reflects learning practice; and 'purposive' testing, which sets a task in imitation of a real exchange. Representative testing uses assessment techniques which enable the student to show what he can do: an exercise in the use of language for assessment purposes which results in judgements like: 'if he can fill in a gap, it is likely that he has a grasp of the structure of the language'. Examples of this kind of test are role play as drama (where both participants know in advance roughly what the content of the exchange is to be), cloze, and dictation. Purposive testing gives the student tasks which he fulfils by using what he has learnt, and this results in judgements like: 'by following instructions related to a map, he has shown he will be able to find his way'. Examples of this kind of test include communicative encounters such as role play which bridges an information gap (when facts or opinions not known before are passed from one participant to another), extracting information from a text and using it for another purpose, letter writing, using the telephone, and solving a problem. Representative testing is interested in the quality of the language used by the student to achieve the aim of the test; purposive testing is interested in the effectiveness of the communication in developing rapport between the people involved in the exchange. This definition separates communicative testing from the testing of language manipulation, but both can be used to assess proficiency.

7.2 Commentary

In this specification (Figure 34), the skills are more mixed than elsewhere, which is the direct result of applying the language to purposes. There are again problems in defining objectives and content because the variations allowed within the formats suggested are limited only by the context, and there are no set expected responses. The best solution to these problems is to try out draft materials in class to establish how well they work as exchanges, and to discover what language is generated by carrying them out. The tests are all separate, like diagnostic tests (Figure 12), and so the scoring systems are independent: there is no need to arrange any particular weighting. Nevertheless, most of the tests as described are quite short and are therefore better suited to informal classroom use. Some of them (for example, *T: transfer*) could be extended to improve reliability for more formal assessments by giving more information for the same pictures or other stimulus material, but it is probably better to add another test in the same format, (taking the opportunity perhaps to vary the content) and then the two scores can be added into a composite score for the test type. Since most of these tests will be similar to classwork, the students' understanding of the rubric can be improved if the teacher tries out the system (but not the same content) beforehand. This will familiarise the students with the procedures and provide material for learning, while providing the teacher with practice in test setting.

Figure 34 Proficiency tests: a specification

Objectives (reference to future uses)
    Student can
1 (for example) learn more of a subject in which he is already knowledgeable through the medium of the language
2 (for example) survive as a visitor in a country in which the language is spoken . . .
3 . . .

Skills†

        test T: *L2*/v/t/W2 transfer
        test U: *L2*/v/a follow instructions
        test V: v/*S2*/L2//L2/*a*/S2 give advice††
        test W: L2/*S2* appropriate responses
        test X: L2/S2/s/W2/R2/W2 sequence

test Y: R2/*S2*/*L2*//R2/*L2*/*S2* role play††
test Z: R2/S2/*L2*/v/s (times four) problem solving

Content
language: (for example) technical terms; simple present passive
             constructions (process); directions (left, right, straight
             on); imperatives . . .

subjects: (for example) forestry; walking; driving . . .

Formats
test T: listening text, 400 words, 20 pictures (20 minutes)
test U: listening text, 250 words, map, draw routes (10 minutes)
test V: diagram, describe as necessary for partner to draw, make
           object (5 minutes)
test W: listening text, 20 sections, 30 words each, respond to 20
           situations (5 minutes)
test X: listening text, 200 words, reply, look up reference, write note
           (10 minutes)
test Y: cue/role cards, carry out transaction (5 minutes)
test Z: information sheets, realia, instructions, answer sheet, agree a
           plan of action (group) (15 minutes)

Rubrics explanation may be needed in native language; if new to
students, demonstration needed beforehand

Materials
student: test sheets
teacher: tape and playback equipment; realia; equipment for action
            (tests V, Y) and for discussion (test Z); key sheets and
            marking schemes; scoring sheets for speaking

Marking
test T: 20 marks (20 items × 1)
test U: 15 marks (15 items × 1)
test V: 40 marks (20 actions × 2)
test W: 40 marks (20 responses × 2)
test X: 40 marks (20 steps × 2)
test Y: 40 marks (20 transactions × 2)
test Z: 40 marks (20 exchanges × 2)

(each test to be totalled separately; no composite score for all tests
together)

---

†For key to coding of skills, see Figure 4, page 19.
†† The double line (//) separates two student participants.

7.3 Setting the tests

T: TRANSFER

This test type is particularly suitable for university or polytechnic students (which is the reason why the example given in Figure 35 is so difficult and specialised), but the same principle can of course be applied to easier material. The principle is that a passage is spoken (preferably not read from a script but based on notes) and the student relates the information given to the pictorial form on his test sheet, identifying which of a series of pictures is referred to by each statement. The same technique can be applied to diagrams of various kinds (graphs, pie charts, Venn diagrams, histograms) according to which are appropriate for the subject. There should always be more pictures or diagrams than statements, so that the last few identifications cannot be made by elimination. Advantages of this test type are that it does not involve any understanding or production of the written language, except a letter or a name, and that the marking is objective. Further examples of the technique, and the rationale behind it, are given in McEldowney 1976.

Figure 35   Test T: transfer – tapescript and test sheet

Notes for lecture. Omit one system altogether from the account.

SYSTEMS OF SILVICULTURE are depicted. In clear-cutting with natural regeneration (*a*) a stand of trees is entirely cut down in a given area. Regeneration of the forest may occur through the natural fall of seeds from trees that remain standing near the clear-cut area. In clear-cutting with planting (*b*) a cleared site may be prepared for the planting of genetically improved seedlings, which grow into a pure stand of even age. The forest is thinned at intervals and treated with fire, fertilizers, herbicides or pesticides as needed. In the shelterwood system (*c*) a stand is cut in such a way that trees remain in the area to provide seed and shelter for a period of years and thereby to make regeneration fairly certain. Once the new growth is established the overstory is removed to leave a young stand of even age. The selection system (*d*) relies on the maintenance of a mixed stand of uneven age and trees that are more or less shade-tolerant. In the proposed short-rotation method, a variety of the coppice system (*e*), trees that grow rapidly and regenerate by sprouting would be intensively cultivated and harvested by machines on rotations as short as two years. The harvested trees would be converted into wood chips for fuel or chemicals.

Listen to the lecture on different systems of silviculture. The pictures are not in the right order. Write A1, A2, A3 and B1, B2, B3 and so on in the squares to show which pictures go together.

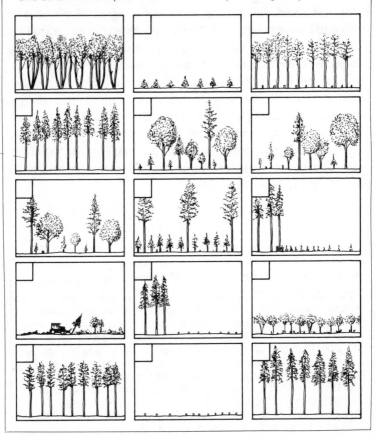

U: FOLLOW INSTRUCTIONS

This is similar in format to *T: transfer* but assesses understanding of instructions rather than of information. In this example (Figure 36) the student is to trace on a map the route he hears from a tape

Figure 36   Test U: follow instructions – tapescript and test sheet

Rubric (also on tape): Here is a map of Croydon. A friend is telling you how to get to two different places. Listen to the tape and then draw lines along the roads on the map to show where he is telling you to go.

'If you are coming by train, get out at East Croydon Station. Outside the station, turn right and walk towards the roundabout. Go under the pedestrian subway and come out at the Park Hill Road exit. Turn right down Park Hill Road; go straight on at the next crossroads; then turn right at the bottom of the hill into Coombe Road. The Teachers' Centre is only a few hundred yards down the road, on the right.

If you are coming later, by car, I shall be at home. Come down the A235, which is called London Road. When you have passed the General Hospital and West Croydon station, you will come into a one-way system. Go straight on at the crossroads by the station, down North End. You will then have to turn left into George Street. Get over into the right hand lane at once and turn right into Park Lane. Go round the big roundabout at the end of the flyover and turn right into Coombe Road. Take the second turning left and my house is opposite the car park, halfway down South End.'

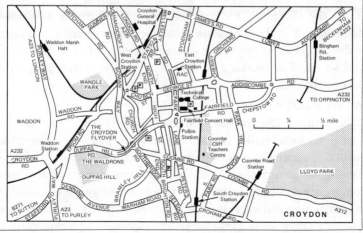

recording. Further routes could be devised without much difficulty and the same map used over and over again for different forms of the test. The marking gives credit for a correct start, each correct change of direction and a correct end. The main problem here, however, is that a missed turning may result in several marks lost. (Perhaps this is justified by considering the difficulty and delay the equivalent error would cause in real life.)

V: GIVE ADVICE

This is a test for a pair of students, one of whom talks much more than the other, so that it should be done twice with the roles reversed. The advice given by the leading student can be anything from authoritative instructions to a discussion resolving uncertainty, but in every case the advice should be about some physical activity. The examples given (Figure 37) begin with a Tangram. Either the speaker can have a key to the pattern he is describing, in which case the language content is instruction and request for clarification, or the puzzle can be done by both students together, and then the language content is question and answer, and suggestion and disagreement. Other possibilities include Origami (though the instructing student has to understand the diagrams and try out the procedure in advance), describing a pattern or object for the other student to draw, instructing him in physical movement from a series of drawings, and so on. The marking of this test requires preparation and practice (see Chapter 8).

W: APPROPRIATE RESPONSES

This example (Figure 38) is drawn directly from the ARELS Certificate Examination (see list of addresses, page 139). The three ARELS examinations (Preliminary, Certificate and Diploma) consist of a series of tests of 'all appropriate verbal and comprehension skills' which are taken in a language laboratory: only listening and speaking are involved. The sample given here covers a fairly wide range of short responses, and this variety

Figure 37 Test V: give advice – activities

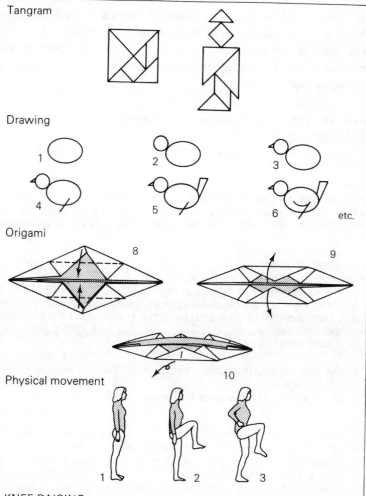

Tangram

Drawing

1

2

3

4

5

6   etc.

Origami

8

9

10

Physical movement

1

2

3

KNEE RAISING
1 Stand straight-backed, with feet together and hands at your sides.
2 Raise right knee fully; repeat with left leg; raise each 5–10 times.
3 For variation, try the same exercise with your hands on your hips.

should be maintained in versions of the test written for particular groups of students. There is no need to record the stimulus utterances unless they are intended for use in the language laboratory, in which case it may be simpler to obtain authentic examples of past examinations direct from ARELS. The simplest method is for the teacher to give the stimulus, as in the usual speaking test.

Figure 38 Test W: appropriate responses – tapescript

SECTION ONE
In this section we test your ability to use the everyday language of common situations.

Part One
First you will hear six remarks which might be made to you in various situations when you are using your English. Some are questions and some are comments. After each one reply in a natural way. Here is an example to help you.
    'Sorry to keep you waiting.'
    'That's all right.'
Now, are you ready? Here is the first.

1 Hasn't it been a marvellous summer!   (SIX SECONDS)
2 Do you know if the banks are open on Saturdays? (SIX SECONDS)
3 I'd love one of those cream cakes, but I really shouldn't. I'm on a strict diet.   (EIGHT SECONDS)
4 What a super pair of boots! Where did you get them?
                                                          (EIGHT SECONDS)
5 I've been ringing his number all day and it's always engaged. I just don't know *what* to do.   (EIGHT SECONDS)
6 Do you mind if I use your phone to call my office in New York?
                                                          (EIGHT SECONDS)

Part Two
Now you will hear fourteen situations in which you might find yourself. Say what it seems natural to say in each situation. Ready?

7 Someone you have recently met shows you a photograph of his three little children. What do you say?   (EIGHT SECONDS)
8 You want to get a packet of cigarettes from a slot machine but you don't have the right change for the machine. There is an old lady standing nearby. What do you say to her?   (EIGHT SECONDS)
9 You are spending a few weeks in a town in Britain. You would like to use the town library while you are there. You go into the library and speak to the girl at the information desk. What do you say?
                                                          (TEN SECONDS)

10 Some friends ask you to go with them to an international folk song evening. They tell you that everyone who goes to it has to sing a song from his own country to entertain the others. What do you say?

(TEN SECONDS)

11 Two days ago you promised to post a letter for a friend. You have just found the letter, still in your coat pocket. What do you say to your friend, who is with you and has seen the letter too.

(EIGHT SECONDS)

12 You are at an international conference and it is coffee break time. There is a man talking a language which you do not recognise. You want to talk to him. What do you say to him? (SIX SECONDS)

13 You are staying in a hotel. It is late at night and you are reading in bed. Suddenly the light over the bed goes out. You telephone room service. What do you say? (EIGHT SECONDS)

14 A man you work with, Fred Smith, has just come back from his summer holidays. What do you say to him when you see him?

(EIGHT SECONDS)

15 You are leaving the English family you have been staying with and going back to your own country. What do you ask the family to do with any letters which come for you? (EIGHT SECONDS)

16 You are listening to a lecture and taking notes. About half-way through the lecture you run out of paper. There is a girl sitting near you who is also making notes. What do you say to her?

(SIX SECONDS)

17 There are two good films on at the local cinema, but you have only got time to go and see one of them. You know a good friend of yours has seen both of these films. What do you ask him?

(EIGHT SECONDS)

18 Two years ago you knew a girl called Mary Smith. She was a typist in your office. You have not seen her for more than a year. One day you see her in the street. She has a young man with her and she is carrying a baby. What do you say to her? (TEN SECONDS)

19 A friend, but not a good friend, asks if he can borrow some of your records for a party he is giving. You have not been invited to this party and you know he is not particularly careful. Say no, but nicely.

(TEN SECONDS)

20 The car you have just hired breaks down half a mile from the pick-up point. You ring the office. What do you say? (TWELVE SECONDS)

SECTION TWO

In this section we test your intonation, stress, rhythm, pronunciation and other details of the way you speak.

Please look at your reading passage. Your friend Bob is telephoning you to ask about British Rail Student Railcards. You will hear Bob's voice on the tape and you must read the part marked *CANDIDATE*. You have two minutes to study the passage before you start reading. You may write on it if you like. Remember, you will have to read the part marked *CANDIDATE*.

Bob: Hello, it's Bob here. I wonder if you can help me.

CANDIDATE: I will if I can. What is it you want? (SIX SECONDS)

Bob: Well, there's a girl staying next door to me, who's going to College next September, and she was asking today about cheap rail fares for students. There's a special card, isn't there? . . .

X: SEQUENCE

In this type of test the student needs to use the four language skills in one of a number of possible sequences to complete a task. (For the first time in all the test types discussed so far there is an equal balance between the skills, so that none is in italics in the specification.) A fairly straightforward example would be telephone/notes/information retrieval/written message. In this sequence the student first receives a request or is given information by the teacher or by another student. This is done verbally (without eye contact and the help of gesture) so as to represent, for example, a telephone conversation. He clarifies details and makes notes on what he has heard, and then looks up supplementary facts in some kind of reference material (a file or a directory). Finally, he writes a message combining the particulars he has gathered together. This simulates a possible sequence for someone who works in an office, and is derived from a similar test in examinations in German and French for business studies (Phillips 1978). A possible content for this sequence is given in Figure 39. Other variations might be: information about entertainment from the radio linked to printed programmes for the week or to the local newspaper, followed by a postcard to a friend who is coming on a visit; or a message in writing (letter, telegram) which requires clarification by telephone (perhaps recorded information, so that the teacher or another student is not needed) followed by a written confirmation. These sequences should be based on authentic material, but if this cannot be obtained in the original it can often be found reproduced in course books or in comprehension exercises (for example Thomas 1977, Davies and Whitney 1980).

Figure 39 Text X: sequence — outline of material

1 Telephone call:
  send off broken part (of bicycle, car, sewing machine . . .) to address dictated.
2 Look up in GPO directory/leaflet how to wrap it up; no sacking available.
3 Write note for someone going to shops asking him to get sacking, plus strong paper and string.
  Also ask him to post it (urgent), and give the address.

Maps, plans, drawings, etc.

These should be enclosed in strong cardboard tubes, reinforced if necessary with a rigid rod inside the roll.

Metal castings, etc.

Metal castings should be securely tied in a wrapping of some textile such as hessian or sacking before being placed in a stout wooden or fibreboard container with enough packing material to prevent all movement, and provide a 1 inch margin of packing on all sides.

Musical instruments.

Musical instruments should be packed in stout boxes with sufficient soft packing to prevent movement and damage through jolting. The cases supplied for carrying do not afford adequate protection. The bridges of stringed instruments should be removed and packed separately. For valuable instruments it is advisable to consult a professional packer.

Nuts, bolts, small machine parts, etc.

Because of their relatively heavy weight, nuts, bolts, and small machine parts are liable to burst all but the strongest packing. Wrap in hessian or sacking, tie with string, and place in a strong box, with enough cushioning material to prevent movement.

Paints, enamels, varnishes and kindred substances

Flashpoints over 150°F (66°C): pack as for liquids.
Flashpoints between 90°F (32°C) and 150°F (66°C): not more than one quart may be sent in a single. . . .

The problems with this test type are the rubric and the marking. The sequence should run from one event to the next without the student knowing in advance what the content is to be, but he has to have some overall idea of what he is going to be asked to do. The best solution is not to attempt the sequence in test form until it has been established as a learning technique in class. The marking relates to defined steps in the sequence, which means that the content has to be carefully worked out in advance. The marking system is best done on a $1+1$ basis, statement by statement (see page 114).

Y: ROLE PLAY

This is such a common teaching technique that little need be said here about the principles behind it. The essence of it is to provide students with information which they must use in exchanges with each other. Revell (1979) defines a role play as 'an individual's spontaneous behaviour reacting to others in a hypothetical situation'. It was suggested earlier (page 92) that role plays can be approached either as drama, with participants knowing in advance roughly what the content is to be, or as bridging an information gap, when the participants need to find out something they do not already know in order to carry out the exercise. Two other points are important from the point of view of assessment. Firstly, the student can either play himself in a realistic situation which (by definition) he is not actually in at the moment, or he can take the part of someone else in a fictional situation which he may or may not encounter at some future date. This is not the same as the distinction (made by Littlewood and quoted by Revell) between the various roles people play according to the varying circumstances of their daily lives. Secondly, more than two people may be involved, and the teacher does not have to be one of them.

Two kinds of problem can be set for the assessment of role plays: simulations, in which the student is required to use language for the kinds of purpose that he will need it for in real life (such as obtaining information, buying tickets); and puzzles, which make the student use language to communicate in more general ways (explaining, asking for confirmation, disagreeing).

One of the dangers with role plays as tests is that they can be too well rehearsed in learning, so that the exchange runs on a fixed track and there is no real evidence that the students could cope with a similar situation in real life, where the answers would not come pat out of the textbook. This suggests that at some point in the role play things should go wrong for the participants, so that they have to say something other than the standard reply.

The example given in Figure 40 is part of the speaking test from the Council of Europe's draft specimen test for Threshold level English. The five entries on the teacher's guide show the number of the question (E = examiner, C = candidate), the question to be asked and suggested answers; the objectives for each question; suggested prompts, and notes and instructions for the teacher. This is a structured version of a role play test and a more informal system might be more appropriate within a school. There should be no difficulty at all in finding suggestions for role plays which can be converted into tests, but the teacher should check carefully that the ones he chooses do relate quite specifically to the language use that he wants to assess. Examples will be found in Maley & Duff 1978, Watcyn Jones 1978, Revell 1979 and Rixon 1981, among many others.

Z: PROBLEM SOLVING

Other test types for proficiency have involved teacher and student or two students or a group of students, but the problem-solving test must be done by a group of between three and six students. The principle is that each of the students is given some information (a timetable, a map, an advertisement, publicity material, postcards) and between them they have an instruction sheet and an answer sheet. The aim of the exercise is to plan some

Figure 40 Test Y: role play – teacher's guide

Test guide		Answer content	Prompt	Notes
E	Thank you. Now *you* are going to ask *me* some questions. You are in a Tourist Information Office in London. I am the man/woman behind the desk. Here are some things which are going on in London, and here is a £5 note. *Choose one* of the things on the paper and			check understanding: talk slowly, repeating and explaining with other words and gestures if necessary. Give C events list & £5 note – real one if available
16E	ask me about times of starting and the cost of *two tickets*	action/event, question		repeat if needed
16C	... (what time does the pub walk/do the concerts start? ...)			
17E	At 7.30 every evening and also at 3 in the afternoon on Saturdays. You can get tickets here if you like.	action/event, question	*the tickets are not very expensive/quite cheap*	
17C	... (how much is it for 2 tickets/what do 2 tickets cost? ...)			

18E	Tickets cost £2 for evenings and £1 for Saturday afternoons. Which day do you want to go?	request	
18C	... (Monday evening/Saturday afternoon ...)		
19E	Here you are.	correcting: accept any verbal protest – more than facts needed for 'communication' mark	*you wanted them for x (wrong time/day) didn't you?*	give wrong tickets: if prompt fails, use gesture
19C	... (I'm sorry, but these are wrong/this isn't right ...)			
E	Oh, I'm so sorry, here are the right ones. That will be £4/£2.			
C	... (offers £5 note)			
20E	I'm afraid I haven't any pound notes. I shall have to give you it all in ten pence pieces.	forgiveness/in-difference: accept any acceptance, willing or not – yes alone not enough	*is that all right?*	use real 10p pieces if available
20C	... (that's all right/it doesn't matter ...)			
E	Here you are			

E = examiner
C = candidate

activity such as a day trip or a holiday: the minimum might be an evening out which has to be reconciled with conflicting diaries and different interests, and the maximum a full simulation exercise in its widest sense (see Jones 1980). Between these extremes the problem-solving activity could include abstract problems such as working out the sequence of operations involved in the manufacture of a car, or semantic problems such as the arrangement of a narrative in its correct order from sections shared out among the students. (A listening version of this coordination exercise is *Listening Links*, Geddes and Sturtridge 1978.)

It is essential that the students have done similar exercises before and that they accept the rules of the game, especially the rule that they do not use their native language. It is also important that they understand the aim of the exercise, which is not necessarily to find the 'right' answer as quickly as possible (in fact, there may be no right answer at all) but to work towards agreement from conflicting starting points. The procedure covers large areas of language use, from gist reading to close argument, and all students have to contribute because each of them has some information which the others need in order to come to a decision.

The assessment should ideally be made on the effectiveness of the language used by each student, which means that a time sequence method is probably the most appropriate. This does mean, however, that the test has to be tried out as an exercise several times before it is used for assessment, in order that the teacher as test setter can build up some experience to support the content of the mark scheme.

Figure 41 shows part of the material which could be used for a test based on a prospective visit to the Edinburgh Festival, and would need supplementing with, for example, train and air time-tables, diaries, postcards of places which could be visited and other publicity material. Realia should be used wherever possible.

Figure 41 Test Z: problem solving

8 Marking

8.1 Objective

From the marking point of view, tests fall into one of two categories: objective or subjective. The objective test has only one correct answer, but the subjective test may result in a range of possible answers, some of which are more acceptable than others. It is not really the tests which are objective or subjective, but the systems by which they are marked.

Objective marking is possible with multiple-choice and true/false formats such as *A: scripted speech* and *O: text and argument*, and also with exact cloze and matching formats like *T: transfer* and *N: unscripted speech*. In all these tests, a list of the keys gives the only correct answers. (In actual fact, the tests are not as objective as this might suggest, since a great deal of judgement has been used in developing and setting them, from the specification to the acceptance or rejection of items at the review stage.) A multiple-choice test is usually pretested, which means that it is tried out on a sample of the students it was written for and the results looked at to see if the items and the test as a whole are consistent. It is this consistency of items and tests in sorting out the students into approximately the same rank order that is called reliability. If the test is reliable enough (another judgement), the next problem is to be sure that it is valid: that what the test assesses so consistently is what it was intended to assess. A multiple-choice test can be very consistent, but it may cover a very limited area of the content.

The actual marking is easy: the correct answers are simply added up into a score. The method of counting up depends on whether the students answered directly in a test booklet or on a separate answer sheet. If there are separate answer sheets, the simplest method is to adapt one as a key sheet by marking the correct answers on it and then making a transparent copy, either by hand or by photocopying. This is then used as an overlay which is placed on top of each student's answer sheet in turn. The correct answers are added up and the total is written in the top right hand corner. (The corner of the overlay can be cut off to make this easier.) A transparent sheet is best because it shows up any cases where more than one answer has been given for an item, a response which is always counted as wrong. The simplest source of a transparent sheet is an acetate such as those used on an overhead projector. When the students answer in the test booklet itself, it is not possible to use a single overlay because the answers will appear on several pages. It is possible to make a set of overlays, one for each page, but they are awkward to use and it is better to prepare one sheet with all the keys listed in columns. One column is used for each page of the test booklet, and the solutions are positioned so that each is on the same level as its related item as the pages of the booklet are turned and the key sheet is pulled out sideways from under it, column by column.

8.2 Subjective

Subjective marking is much more problematical. The mark scheme should be thought out at an early stage in the development of the test, since it is in principle a forecast of what the students will produce and so affects what is to be included in the assessment. It is drawn up from experience of teaching but should be tried out on a trial version of the test so that any necessary adjustments can be made.

There are various ways of making judgements about written language. One is simply to put all the answer sheets in rank order, from best to worst, by comparing one with another and sorting them, rather like a hand in a game of cards. This is done by quick scanning rather than detailed reading, but even though it does not take long for each individual script, it is too clumsy a procedure for more than about twenty students at once. However, it does separate them (by definition) from each other, and may be useful for the rapid check of a small amount of writing such as *C: structured writing*. A refinement of this 'global-quality' scaling is to sort the answers into several piles according to different levels of quality, aiming either to put approximately the same number of answers in each pile, or to relate the numbers in each pile to the normal distribution. The former is easier to put into practice, but the latter is more accurate, especially if the pattern is one of nine piles achieved by two stages of sorting, firstly into three piles and then each of these three into three again. (However, an approximately normal distribution is not an appropriate aim for all testing purposes; see page 14.) The principles of this system of grading are given in Ebel (1972: 150) and an explanation of the nine-pile system in Broughton *et al* (1980: 147).

Another system, perhaps the most frequently used, is to assess in categories such as vocabulary, grammar, content and form, allotting, say, five marks to each and awarding a total mark out of twenty. The marker needs considerable practice if he is to apply it consistently (reliably) and, if more than one marker is involved, they should discuss what each of the categories means and what levels they are setting, preferably with samples of scripts, before the marking proper is begun. (The samples could in practice be the first few, which are all re-marked again after the discussion.) It is useful to arrange for one or two markers to check a sample of the scripts afterwards too, but there is rarely enough time for this to be done before the results have to be known. This category system is probably the commonest way of marking essays.

A purely mechanical system of marking continuous written work, such as an essay, is to count off sections of, say, eight words, without taking account of sense, and see what can be given credit: sequences of correct words, vocabulary, verb forms, idioms, phrasal verbs and so on. This system seems very arbitrary but is more reliable than the categories system described above. It needs clearly defined credit points, and teachers new to it need practice in applying it before they have to deal with real scripts. It is useful for marking tests like *P: letter* and *Q: reorientation*. A less arbitrary version is to divide the answer into sense groups. For instance, using the examples given for the second reorientation test (Figure 32), credit would be given for each event included, as represented by the words underlined in the text, by dividing them off into sections with double vertical lines. Anything which is not directly relevant is bracketed and cannot count for the award of further points, except for register (see below). Within the sections, points are given for various elements of language, as the test setter decides, depending on the purpose of the assessment. In the illustration in Figure 42, these elements are tenses (marked *t*), structures (*s*), pronoun (*p*), words not given in the stimulus (underlined) and aspects of register (*r*).

For written text which contains a specified number of events, for example *P: letter*, where the student must make requests and give information, the marking system can be based on communi-

Figure 42   Q: reorientation text 2, marking

```
          r           p       s     t          p
1  (Mr Morgan rang). He asked if he could speak to you.//
       p         p     t  r
   but I told him you weren't in. .//.
     t                          t
2  I telephoned Mr Ward// but he was out.//
   p                t                r                t    r
   I asked if Miss Ward was there,// but Miss Jones said she was not in
   either.//
```

cation and correctness as two separate criteria. One mark is awarded for success in communicating, so the marker asks: 'Would this be understood?' If this mark is awarded, but not otherwise, the marker considers how correct (or, at higher levels, how appropriate) the statement is and awards the other mark accordingly. This system is more reliable than marking by categories (as above), especially if there are a dozen or so statements or communicative acts to be considered. This is because only three marks are possible each time (two, one, zero), whereas with the category system there is more scope for variation and a wider margin of potential marking error. But it can only work with a series of points made or questions answered, and not with a continuous narrative or description, when it is difficult to decide where one statement stops and another starts.

8.3 Dictation

Dictations are usually marked either negatively, by taking one mark off for every error, or more positively by taking groups of between one and six words in the text and awarding marks on the two–one–zero communication-correctness basis or, more severely, demanding absolute accuracy for one mark per group. This is quicker than awarding one point for each word correct right through the dictation, and probably just as reliable.

8.4 Cloze

Cloze and the various kinds of completion test are marked either by giving a mark for the exact word of the original text and no other, or by the 'acceptable' method, which means that judgements have to be made as to what is acceptable (see page 40). Marking by the exact method is objective and very simple provided the mechanics of test sheet, answer sheet and key sheet are properly organised. Indeed, it can be done by anyone who can read handwriting and match word to word, and add up at the end. The acceptable method, however, needs preparation in advance. The test setter will be able to think of several alternative fillers for most gaps, but these will not be enough for a mark scheme and several fluent speakers should be asked to do the test in advance so that a wider variety of fillers can be considered. Decisions, sometimes very difficult ones, then have to be made as to which alternatives are to be counted as acceptable and which must be rejected. The decisions can be complicated by the fact that one filler may affect the acceptability of another. In practice, it is best to reject any alternative about which there is doubt, however unfair this may seem to the more creative student. Another problem is that there will always be some unforeseen alternatives, so that the marker is faced with an occasional individual judgement. But if the pretesting has been reasonably thorough these exceptions to the mark scheme should be fairly rare, and can therefore be counted among the doubtful fillers and rejected.

The third way of marking a cloze test, known as clozentropy, takes the frequency of a large sample of native speakers' fillers as a guide to how much credit should be given for a particular answer. This not only introduces a complicated system of differentiated marking, but is also beyond the scope of most teachers because they do not have enough time or enough native speakers available to put it into practice. In any case, it hardly seems worth the effort when exact marking can produce useful results.

8.5 Speaking

Speaking tests are usually marked either by the category or communication-correctness systems, depending on the structure of the text. As with writing, the latter system can be applied only to a series of statements or events (as found in *F: conversation*). A variation on this one-plus-one marking is to award marks first according to how successfully the student has accomplished the task (for example, *R: speak to pictures, S: talk on topic*) and then to add or deduct marks for the student's use of language in carrying it out. With a maximum of twenty-five, this plus or minus could amount to five marks.

Another system is based on categories of level rather than content. Working with an A to E series of grades, each level can be described in terms of qualities such as 'clear presentation of material', 'clear articulation and vocalisation', 'good vocabulary'. The recommendation accompanying this system is that the marker starts from the middle of grade C, assuming the student to be of average level until he proves otherwise by his performance whereupon he moves up or down the scale accordingly. This system would also be suitable for *R: speak to pictures* or *S: talk on topic*.

Assessing the spoken language used in the various kinds of interaction suggested for proficiency tests, especially with groups of students, is more problematical. Ideally, the way to establish just what language is needed to carry out a role play is to ask native or fluent speakers to do it, tape them, and analyse afterwards what the essential language uses are. For example, it is impossible to tell someone how to make an origami model (see Figure 37) without using the word 'fold', but 'diagonal' can be avoided by saying 'from corner to corner'. In addition, it is possible to specify structures which will necessarily occur (imperatives in the case of the origami activity), and functions which will necessarily be implied (instructing, correcting, confirming). These essentials can then form the criteria for a marking scheme which lays down procedures for how to judge the student's use of them, and which takes no account of the rest of the exchange.

All this, however, may take too long to set up, since it involves several trial runs with the test tasks. A shorter procedure for setting up the mark scheme is to predict from experience what language is likely to occur in a controlled role play, but even this should be tried out with pairs of students as a class exercise to see how correct the predictions are. If fluent or native speakers can be persuaded to try it out as well, there will be a sounder basis for deciding what should be included in the mark scheme and what left out. The important point about setting up the scheme in this way is that it does not attempt to evaluate everything that is said. Once they have been decided upon, the elements which are included in the mark scheme can be assessed in the usual way.

As with other aspects of testing, preparing a mark scheme is a matter of a teacher exercising his judgement as to what is needed for a particular purpose, trying out the result with students, and implementing the scheme only when it is known to work reasonably well.

9 Results

The teacher who wishes to know how well a test has worked, or how the scores it has produced are to be interpreted, needs to know how to deal with some simple statistics. The basis of statistics is that the more often the same event occurs (in the present instance, a score or a set of scores), the more often it is likely to occur again in the future. This means that the higher the number of scores used for the statistical work, the more convincing are the statements that can be made about the tests. In experimental test development work, researchers usually like to try out new tests on about two hundred students before the statistics derived from them can be used as evidence for how good the tests are for the job they were designed to do. The teacher setting a test for his own class may have to try it out several times with different groups of students before he can even approach this figure, but he will want to use the results of his test as soon as he is satisfied that it works well enough for his purposes. Fortunately, he does not need to be very demanding unless he is setting an achievement test that is to be used for important qualification purposes, in which case he will take more time and care over the preparation of it, probably in collaboration with other teachers (see page 64).

The minimum information that the teacher needs to have about his test includes: how it has spread the students out along the range of scores, how difficult or easy it has been for the students who took it, how consistent it has been in its measurements (how reliable), and how accurately it relates to what it is intended to measure (how valid). As mentioned in Chapter 2, a wide spread of scores may not always be the pattern to aim for, since although such a spread is helpful in applying the results of placement and achievement tests, it may not be appropriate for proficiency tests and almost certainly will not be for diagnostic tests. The difficulty of a test is indicated by the average score (more accurately, the arithmetic average, or 'mean'), which is arrived at by adding up all the scores and dividing the total by the number of students taking the test. The reliability of the test is judged by how exactly the same results can be arrived at on different occasions with similar groups of students or from assessment of the same answers by different markers, and therefore depends on repetition of one kind or another. The content validity of the test is assured by the accuracy of the specification, which is why specifications have been given so much emphasis in the preceding chapters. In reviewing the results of a test, the guideline for action is always the occurrence of anything unexpected. If the results are the same as before, or as intended, or reasonable in the circumstances for which the test was designed, the test can be counted as satisfactory. Anything out of line or unforeseen should be investigated.

9.1 Distribution and mean

The first task is to take the total score for each student on the test and record (or tally) it to form the distribution. The distribution is usually represented by a list of figures or by a diagram, but it is fairly simple to produce both at once. Figure 43, shows an analysis for a test of twenty items taken by twenty-five students. The marks which can be obtained for the test as a whole (here anything from zero to twenty) are listed down the left-hand side of a sheet of squared paper and the total score from each student's answer sheet is tallied in turn opposite the relevant number, using an equal amount of horizontal space for each tally. This space can be either a full square or half a square. If there is a large number of students, it is more convenient to group the tallies in fives, four down and one across (⊔⊔⊔). This makes the final totalling quick.

Figure 43 Test analysis sheet 1

Stage A

score (out of 20)	f	x
0		
1		
2		
3		
4		
5		
6	1	6
7		
8	2	16
9		
10	2	20
11	4	44
12	3	36
13	5	65
14	4	56
15	2	30
16	1	16
17		
18	1	18
19		
20		
	N = 25	307

Mean

$\frac{307}{25} = 12.28$ $\underline{12.3}$ (say 12.3)

Standard deviation

$\frac{1}{6}$ of N = 4.16 (say 4)
$\frac{1}{2}$ of N = 12.5
Sum of top $\frac{1}{6}$ (18 + 16 + 15 + 15) = 64
Sum of bottom $\frac{1}{6}$ (6 + 8 + 8 + 10) = 32
difference (top minus bottom) = 32

$\frac{32}{12.5} = 2.56$ $\underline{2.6}$ (say 2.6)

Stage B

score (out of 20)	f	x
0		
1		
2		
3		
4		
5		
6	1	6
7		
8	2	16
9		
10	2	20
11	4	44
12	3	36
13	5	65
14	4	56
15	2	30
16	1	16
17		
18	1	18
19		
20		
	N = 25	307

Mean

$\frac{307}{25} = 12.28$ $\underline{12.3}$ (say 12.3)

Standard deviation

$\frac{1}{6}$ of N = 4.16 (say 4)
$\frac{1}{2}$ of N = 12.5
Sum of top $\frac{1}{6}$ (18 + 16 + 15 + 15) = 64
Sum of bottom $\frac{1}{6}$ (6 + 8 + 8 + 10) = 32
difference (top minus bottom) = 32

$\frac{32}{12.5} = 2.56$ $\underline{2.6}$ (say 2.6)

Figure 43 Test analysis sheet 1

Stage C

	f	x
0		
1		
2		
3		
4		
5		
6	1	6
7		
8	2	16
9		
10	2	20
11	4	44
12	3	36
13	5	65
14	4	56
15	2	30
16	1	16
17		
18	1	18
19		
20		
	N = 25	307
	12.3	

Mean

$\dfrac{307}{25}$ = 12.28 (say 12.3)

Standard deviation

⅙ of N = 4.16 (say 4)
½ of N = 12.5
Sum of top ⅙ (18 + 16 + 15 + 15) = 64
Sum of bottom ⅙ (6 + 8 + 8 + 10) = 32
difference (top minus bottom) = 32

$\dfrac{32}{12.5}$ = 2.56 (say 2.6) 2.6

Stage D

	f	x
0		
1		
2		
3		
4		
5		
6	1	6
7		
8	2	16
9		
10	2	20
11	4	44
12	3	36
13	5	65
14	4	56
15	2	30
16	1	16
17		
18	1	18
19		
20		
	N = 25	307
	12.3	

Mean

$\dfrac{307}{25}$ = 12.28 (say 12.3)

Standard deviation

⅙ of N = 4.16 (say 4)
½ of N = 12.5
Sum of top ⅙ (18 + 16 + 15 + 15) = 64
Sum of bottom ⅙ (6 + 8 + 8 + 10) = 32
difference (top minus bottom) = 32

$\dfrac{32}{12.5}$ = 2.56 (say 2.6) 2.6

The process of carrying out the test analysis is best described in stages. *Stage A* (see Figure 43) is to add up horizontally the number of tallies at each mark and list the totals vertically down the sheet in a column labelled f (for 'frequency'). These frequencies are then totalled at the bottom as a check on the number of students (N) taking the test. This number is of course both the number of students and the number of scores in the analysis. In *Stage B*, each mark is multiplied by its frequency and the result is listed in a column headed X, which is again totalled at the bottom to give all scores for all students. This total is then divided by N (*Stage C*) to arrive at the mean score for the test (M). If the sheet is now turned anticlockwise through ninety degrees and the ends of the last tallies entered on the distribution are joined up vertically, a diagram which shows the spread of scores graphically (a 'histogram') appears, as in Figure 44.

Figure 44   Histogram

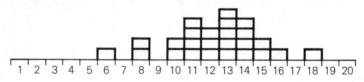

This analysis sheet now contains a considerable amount of useful information. From the frequency distribution an overall picture of the test begins to appear. The numbers in column f show that the lowest score was 6 and the highest 18, which in itself gives an indication of how well the students were separated out by the test. This information is misleading, however, if there are odd scores at either end of the distribution (if the bottom student scored 6 and the next best 13, for example). But the whole distribution shows whether this is so, particularly in its graphic form and when there are large numbers of students. The distribution also shows the relationship between any one score and the rest of the scores for the test, so that instead of just noting that a student scored 14, it is clear that he has done better than seventeen other students in the class but not as well as the top four. The mean score shows how difficult the test was. A high mean, for example, indicates that students found the test easy. The mean is useful in making comparisons with other tests and with other groups of students on the same test, but it has no absolute value of its own. It results from the interaction of the students with the test. Consequently, if the standard of the students is known, the mean will show whether the test was set at the right level; and if the test has already been proved in action with several groups of students at the appropriate level, it will show what standard a new group of students has reached.

9.2 Standard deviation

The above procedures will give the minimum information needed by the teacher to know whether his tests are working in the way he intended, but for more important tests more information is required. The results of a certificated achievement test need to be as accurate as possible, and a similar accuracy is also desirable for placement tests, though the situation here is more informal and any gross misplacements suggested by the test scores should be corrected by the interview (see page 5). As a last resort they can be corrected by moving a student to another class at a future date.

The most useful basis for the next stage of test analysis is the standard deviation (SD), which shows how well the test has separated the students from each other. One consequence of the stability of the normal curve is that the relationship between a score and the number of students achieving it is constant. Figure 44 shows than when the normal curve is divided up into sections corresponding to one SD each, about two thirds of the scores will always fall within plus or minus one SD of the mean (M), and 95 per cent within plus or minus two SDs.

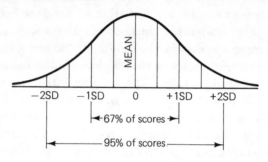

adapted from Ebel (1972: 283)

The importance of this consistency is that it gives a standard with which to compare the spread produced by any test which approximates to the normal curve. The SD of a given test shows not only how relatively spread scores are as compared with the normal curve, but also gives a numerical comparison with tests of a similar kind, (whether the achievement test set at the end of this school year, for example, is spreading the students out to the same extent as last year), so that decisions about the grades to be awarded can be made with more informed judgement. The SD is needed for many calculations related to the analysis of tests, including statistical comparisons such as those required for estimates of reliability and for those aspects of validity which depend on checks with other tests.

A simple (though approximate) way of calculating the SD for a set of scores is to subtract the bottom sixth of the scores from the top sixth and divide the result by half the number of scores (a procedure suggested by Lathrop and quoted by Ebel (1972: 281)). The result of this calculation for the distribution given in Figure 43 is shown in Stage D, and comes out at 2.6. Some indication of what size of variation might be expected in different circumstances is given by a similar calculation in Figure 46, which comes out at 4.2.

Figure 46 Test analysis sheet 2

Score (out of 30)

		f	x
0			
1			
2			
3			
4			
5			
6			
7	I	1	7
8			
9	III	3	27
10	IIIII	5	50
11	IIII	4	44
12	I	1	12
13	I	1	13
14			
15	III	3	45
16	I	1	16
17	I	1	17
18			
19	I	1	19
20	II	2	40
21			
22	I	1	22
23			
24	I	1	24
25			
26			
27			
28			
29			
30			

Reliability

$$r = 1 - \frac{M(n-M)}{ns^2}$$

$$= 1 - \frac{13.4\,(30-13.4)}{30 \times 4.2^2}$$

$$= 1 - \frac{222.4}{529.2}$$

$$= 1 - .42$$

$$= .58 \qquad \underline{.58}$$

Mean

$$\frac{336}{25} = 13.44 \text{ (say 13.4)} \qquad \underline{13.4}$$

Standard deviation

$\frac{1}{6}$ of N = 4.16 (say 4)
$\frac{1}{2}$ of N = 12.5
sum of top $\frac{1}{6}$ (24 + 22 + 20 + 20) = 86
sum of bottom $\frac{1}{6}$ (7 + 9 + 9 + 9) = 34
difference   (top minus bottom) = 52

$$\frac{52}{12.5} = 4.16 \text{ (say 4.2)} \qquad \underline{4.2}$$

9.3 Reliability

To calculate the reliability of a test, the following formula is commonly used:

$$r = 1 - \frac{M(n - M)}{ns^2} \quad \text{(Kuder-Richardson formula 21)}$$

where M is the mean, n is the number of items in the test and s is the SD. Substituting the numbers given in Figure 46, the reliability estimate (r) comes out at .58. This is not an acceptable level for a certified achievement test, which should reach reliability estimates of about .7, but it might be acceptable for a diagnostic test which is to be the basis of class discussion. The same calculation for the scores given in Figure 43 produces an even lower figure. (Those readers who would like to try this calculation themselves will find the figure at the end of this section.) This difference shows that higher levels of reliability are likely with a longer test, because it gives opportunities for a wider range of scores.

More complicated procedures in the statistical treatment of test results are not needed for the language teacher setting tests for his own purposes, but those who want to explore them will find further information on the application of statistical methods to language tests in Allen and Davies 1977. (For a more general discussion of issues in educational measurement, see Ebel 1972.)

The procedures discussed above for calculating the SD and estimating the reliability of a test assume that the spread of scores is similar to that of a normal distribution. Sometimes, however, this is not the case. A diagnostic test may be designed so that nearly all the students answer nearly all of the test correctly, showing that they have grasped what they have been taught and giving clear indications of where they have not. In this case the distribution histogram (Figure 44) and the calculation of the mean (Figure 43) are useful as general indications of spread and difficulty, but more important is information about which items or questions were not answered correctly. An item analysis (see next section) or an inspection of scripts is the first step, but the information gained from these procedures is derived from the interaction of the students and the test, and it is important to find out whether the answers were wrong because the students had not learnt what they were taught or because the test was not asking the right question or was ambiguous in some way. The best way of establishing this is by class discussion of test results.

(The reliability estimate for the test in Figure 43 is .3.)

9.4 Item analysis

The main information to be obtained about individual items (both multiple-choice and true/false) is how difficult they are and how well they sort out the better students from the poorer ones. Pretesting items is often regarded as essential for the more formal testing purposes, because trying them out with students shows how they work in practice, and it is only from this experimentation that bad items can be identified and amended or thrown out. The difficulties about pretesting are that there is often little time available to arrange it separately from other testing and that the students for the pretesting should be a fair sample of those who are to take the test in its final ('operational') form later on. The solution to these problems is to develop the tests gradually, trying out new items (or sets of items) at the same time as established ones, but not scoring them for results until they have been reviewed. The two consequences of this method are that the tests must be in some parallel pattern, perhaps a modular one, so that new and established tests can be slotted into the battery as necessary; and that only a relatively small amount of new material can be introduced at any one sitting of the test. Pretests are less important, however, for diagnostic tests, since the results will probably be discussed in class. The difficulty of an item, known as its 'facility index', is simply the percentage of students who give the right answer. For example, if twenty out of twenty-five students answered an item correctly, the facility index would be $\frac{20}{25}$ = .80, or 80 per cent. The usual aim of test writers is to achieve fairly even and middling facility indices right through the test, ranging from about .40 to about .60. An exception to this rule is the test set on an incline of difficulty (see page 27) but the incline makes no essential difference to the value of the test results for this purpose, provided the easiness and difficulty at either end of the test are not too extreme.

To estimate the discrimination of an item, the total scores of the students on the test are used as a yardstick against which to judge the efficiency of the items. If students who do well on the test as a whole also get a particular item right, and the students who do badly on the test as a whole get it wrong, both test and item are sorting the students out consistently (and therefore reliably). This circular argument is the justification for accepting or rejecting items at the review stage. Some way of contrasting the top and bottom students is therefore needed, and the ideal is to use the top and bottom 27 per cent. This has been found, experimentally, to be the best compromise between the greatest contrast (highest and lowest scores) and the largest number of comparisons. Working out 27 per cent, however, is not necessary for small groups of students, and for up to forty it is enough to divide the distribution in half and use the two sub-groups to contrast the top and bottom students' performances. When there are more than forty students it takes less time if the top and bottom thirds of the distribution are used, and the middle third left out of the analysis.

In terms of the data given in Figure 46, therefore, the distribution is divided in half at scores 11 and 12, and since there is an odd number of students (twenty-five), one of the answer sheets which scored 11 should be taken out. The answer sheets are then sorted into two equal piles according to their total scores, 12 and up into one pile and 11 and below into the other. There will be twelve answer sheets in each pile. The answers given by each student in the 'top' pile to each item are then tallied onto an item analysis sheet (Figure 47). The answers in the 'bottom' pile are tallied on the same analysis sheet, but in a different colour or in a different slot, so that the two sets of tallies are not confused. Once a rhythm of working has been established the tallying does not take as long as might be expected, and it can be speeded up considerably if two people share the task, one calling out the answers and the other tallying. At the end of the tallying the total number in each box can be written in a corner and ringed for ease of reference. Finally, a ring is drawn round the tallies for the keys so that they are clearly identified for the next stage of the analysis.

The facility index of the item is the sum of the two sets of tallies for the key, divided by the number of students, and this can be entered down one side of the analysis sheet. In Figure 46, the key for item 1 is A, which was chosen by 7 'tops' and 3 'bottoms', equalling 10 altogether, and dividing this by 24 gives .42. (This way of calculating the facility index can be used for the top and bottom thirds system too: although it is not quite accurate it will be near enough for the comparative difficulty of the items to be assessed.)

The item's discrimination is judged by comparing the number of tallies appearing in the key slots for top and bottom groups. The discrimination index is arrived at by subtracting the number of correct answers in the bottom group from the number of correct answers in the top group and dividing the result by the number of students in one of the groups (half the total number of students involved):

$$D = \frac{\text{correct T} - \text{correct B}}{\frac{1}{2}N}$$

In Figure 47, the discrimination index for item 1 is $\frac{7-3}{12} = .33$. For item 7, it is $\frac{9-3}{12} = .50$. The index should reach about .3 if the item is

Figure 47 Item analysis sheet

| Test | | | | | | | Date | | |
| Class | | | | | | | N students | | |

item \ option		A	B	C	D	no answer	check total	facility	discrimination
1	T	7	3	2			12	.42	.33
	B	3	3	4	2		12		
2	T	2	9		1		12	.63	.25
	B	2	6	1	3		12		
3	T	3	2	3	4		12	.25	.17
	B	4	1	2	2	3	12		
4	T	2	3	1	4	2	12	.29	.08
	B	3	4	3	1	1	12		
5	T	4	7			1	12	.50	.17
	B	3	5	1		3	12		
6	T	2		2	5	3	12	.29	− .25
	B	3		5	2	2	12		
7	T	3			9		12	.50	.50
	B	4	3	2	3		12		
8	T	5	3	2	2		12		
	B	4	3			5	12		
9	T		12				12		
	B	3	8	1			12		

10	T	2	2	6	2		12	
	B	3	3	4	2		12	
11	T	12					12	
	B	10		2			12	
12								

The last two columns for items 8 to 11 have been left blank for readers to work out the facility index and discimination index for themselves.

discriminating effectively, but higher values are better. Items 2 to 6 in Figure 47 are therefore not good enough statistically speaking, though some of them could be retained in the test if there were other good reasons for doing so (see below).

A useful item should have at least 5 per cent (one in twenty) of the students choosing each distractor, but this level will often not be achieved with low numbers of students. In addition, the distractors should be chosen more often by students in the bottom group than those in the top group, as in Items 1 and 7. Conversely, the key should be chosen more often by students in the top group, as in Items 2 and 9, among others. The pattern of responses represented by the tallies will show which of the items need revising, either because the distractors are not working (Items 5 and 9), or because too many 'poor' students get them right (Item 6), or because the responses of both 'good' and 'poor' students are scattered haphazardly over all of the options (Item 4), or are concentrated on two of them, indicating that there was ambiguity about the key (Item 5).

It should be noted in passing that the data given in Figure 46 is entirely fictional, and such a variety of patterns is not likely to occur in reality. In fact, these results would indicate that the test had been a thoroughly bad one!

It is important to remember that the figures resulting from item analysis should not be taken by themselves as evidence for decisions about the quality of items, particularly if student numbers are low (say, twenty-five or less). In most cases, the analysis will suggest what might be done to improve the item, either by making the key less obvious or replacing one of the distractors. But when the item relates to something which is important in the specification, it should be tried again, even if the figures are rather poor: it may work better next time.

9.5 Follow-up

Detailed feedback for students is clearly vital in the case of diagnostic tests, since it is the whole point of the assessment. However, in this case it is the content of the test, not the resulting figures, which needs discussing. Discussion of content is also useful for proficiency tests, depending on their purpose. If they are used diagnostically, detail is more important than if they are used as assessments of achievement. The results of an achievement test are best issued as grades, and when the test material is secure, there can be no discussion in class afterwards unless there are several forms of the test or a new form is set for every sitting. There is no need for the results of placement tests to be discussed with the students.

Grading decisions for achievement tests depend on the standards to be set, how the distribution compares with that of previous sittings of the test, and also where the natural breaks in the distribution occur. The distribution on which the grading is done will of course be the one produced by the total scores on the battery of tests, not by individual subtests. But the statistics for the subtests should also be compared with those produced on previous occasions, because if they are very different, the weighting of the tests will be altered. If one component produces markedly different figures from before, it should be investigated and an adjustment made if necessary before the scores are added up for grading. The most important consideration is to keep the standard as constant as possible, in fairness to the students.

The value of all the calculations described above is comparative. The value in knowing that the mean score of a test is 13.4 or its reliability .89 lies in how far these figures can be related to the purpose of the test (what is good for a diagnostic test may be bad for achievement), to other tests of the same kind (what was considered acceptable last time?), and to other students' performance on the same test (is this class doing as well in the course at this point as the last class did?). The 'size' of these quantities (for example, how 'good' is .75?) is a matter of experience over time, which builds up eventually into good judgement.

Conclusion

Several themes have run through this book, some of which have been repeated rather often in different ways. But it is perhaps worth attempting a final summary of them here. The first is that the teacher has the ultimate responsibility for deciding what he will test and how he will do it, or indeed, whether to test at all. He is influenced by the aims and needs of the students he is teaching, the course book he is using, the demands of the school and the system and so on, and must therefore devise tests to fit these conditions. This is why the examples given in this book are mainly incomplete: their purpose is to show what the various formats of test look like and what they can contain, but not to serve as models to be used directly for any group of students.

The second theme is that the best basis for setting valid tests is to ask questions at every stage, but especially at the beginning of the test development process, so that the specification is as clear a statement as possible of why the assessment is being made, what it will contain and what the consequences are for teaching, learning and administration.

Thirdly, the statistical work on scores gives support and guidance to the teacher's decisions but does not tell him what to do. If an item has a lower level of discrimination than is recommended, for example, this does not mean that it is automatically rejected.

No one person can write a test by himself, even if he puts it aside for a few days and comes back to revise it later. If he does this he will certainly find all kinds of errors and inconsistencies which he had not noticed as he worked the test out in detail, but this is no substitute for the comments of an interested colleague, who will see the test material from a different viewpoint and will point out ambiguities and possibilities for error which the test writer cannot see: he is too committed to his idea and has too detailed a view of it by the time he has worked it out.

It is very helpful to collect possible test material for future use, just as promising teaching material is collected and hoarded. After the test has been tried out, a file should be started which contains all the materials needed (test sheets and booklets, answer sheets, tapes, pictures and so on) and also a brief record of the use of the test and the results, including notes on possible improvements before the next sitting. In this way a set of tests will build up over a period and will gradually provide more and more scope for various kinds of assessment. (Helpful suggestions about systems for filing material, in a different context, are given in Rixon 1981.)

Finally, one of the greatest virtues in a test writer is patience. It is unusual for any test when it is first used to work as well as the writer hoped, and revisions must be accepted as inevitable. But the test will improve with use and revision, and the test writer will improve with experience. The main problem in writing tests is to steer a middle way between putting together a test which the writer feels is more or less good enough, and taking endless trouble to get the test absolutely right, which may mean that no new test appears at all. The difficulty is to put into practice the right balance of realism and enthusiasm.

Bibliography

Alexander L G, *Mainline Progress A and B*, Teacher's Book, (London: Longman, 1974). (Also Student's Book, 1973.)

Alexander L G, Stannard Allen W, Close R A & O'Neill R J, *English Grammatical Structure*, (London: Longman, 1975).

Allen J P B & Davies A, *Testing and Experimental Methods: The Edinburgh Course in Applied Linguistics*, Vol 4, (London: OUP, 1977).

Bowen B M, *Look Here! A Visual Aids Handbook for Language Teachers*, (London: Macmillan, 1982).

Broughton G, Brumfit C, Flavell R, Hill P & Pincas A, *Teaching English as a Foreign Language*, 2nd ed, (London: Routledge & Kegan Paul, 1980).

Burniston C, *Creative Oral Assessment*, (Oxford: Pergamon, 1968).

Carroll B J, *Testing Communicative Performance*, (Oxford: Pergamon, 1980).

Cohen A D, *Testing Language Ability in the Classroom*, (Rowley, Mass: Newbury House, 1980).

Coles M & Lord B, *Access to English: Open Road*, Teacher's Book, (Oxford: OUP, 1978). (Also Student's Book.)

Crystal D & Davy D, *Advanced Conversational English*, (London: Longman, 1975).

Davies A, (Ed), *Language Testing Symposium*, (London: OUP, 1968).

Davies A, 'Language Testing', survey article in *Language Teaching & Linguistics: Abstracts*, Vol II Nos 3 & 4 1978.

Davies E & Whitney N, *Reasons for Reading*, (London: Heinemann, 1980).

Davies S & West R, *The Pitman Guide to English Language Examinations for Overseas Candidates*, (London: Pitman, 1981).

Ebel R L, *Essentials of Educational Measurement*, (Englewood Cliffs, NJ: Prentice Hall, 1972).

Geddes M & Sturtridge G, *Listening Links*, (London: Heinemann, 1978).

Harris D P, *Testing English as a Second Language*, (New York: McGraw-Hill, 1969).

Heaton J B, *Writing English Language Tests*, (London: Longman, 1975).

Jones K, *Simulations — A Handbook for Teachers*, (London: Kogan Page, 1980).

Lado R, *Language Testing*, (London: Longman, 1961).

McClafferty J, *A Guide to Examinations in English for Foreign Students*, 2nd ed, (London: Hamish Hamilton, 1975).

McEldowney P L, *Test in English (Overseas): the position after ten years*, (Manchester: Joint Matriculation Board, 1976).

Maley A & Duff A, *Drama Techniques in Language Learning*, (Cambridge: CUP, 1978).

Morrow K, 'Communicative Language Testing: Revolution or Evolution?', in Brumfit C J & Johnson K, (Eds), *The Communicative Approach to Language Teaching*, (Oxford: OUP, 1979).

Oller J W, *Language Tests at School*, (London: Longman, 1979).

Phillips D, (Ed), *Continuation German: Report of the Oxford-BP German Project 1977–78*, (Oxford: University of Oxford Department of Educational Studies, 1978).

Revell J, *Teaching Techniques for Communicative English*, (London: Macmillan, 1979).

Rixon S, *How to Use Games in Language Teaching*, (London: Macmillan, 1981).

Thomas B J, *Practical Information*, (London: Arnold, 1977).

Underwood M, *What a Story!*, (Oxford: OUP, 1976).

Valette R M, *Modern Language Testing*, 2nd ed, (New York: Harcourt Brace Jovanovich, 1977).

Van Ek J A, *The Threshold Level for Modern Language Learning in Schools*, (London: Longman, 1977).

Van Ek J A & Alexander L G, *Threshold Level English*, (Oxford: Pergamon, 1980).

Watcyn-Jones P, *Act English*, (Harmondsworth: Penguin, 1978).

Widdowson H G, *Teaching Language as Communication*, (Oxford: OUP, 1978).

Wright A, *Visual Materials for the Language Teacher*, (London: Longman, 1976).

Wright A, Betteridge B & Buckby M, *Games for Language Learning*, (Cambridge: CUP, 1979).

Useful addresses

British Council (ELTS)
10 Spring Gardens
London SW1

The Association of Recognised English Language Schools
125 High Holborn
London WC1V 6QA

Centre for Information on Language Teaching and Research
20 Carlton House Terrace
London SW1Y 5AP

Institute of Linguists
24a Highbury Grove
London N5 2EA

Royal Society of Arts
18 Adam Street
London WC2N 6AJ

Glossary

battery   A set of tests which make a series of assessments of different skills, allowing an overall judgement to be made about a student's standing or level (see page 23).

discrimination The spread of scores produced by a test, or the extent to which a test separates students from one another on a range of scores from high to low. Also used to describe the extent to which an individual multiple-choice item separates the students who do well on the test as a whole from those who do badly (see page 13).

distractors See *item*.

distribution A representation, either as a list of scores or as a graph, of the pattern of scores from high to low (see page 14).

expectancy grammar A term used by Oller and others to describe a speaker's knowledge of the language which allows him to plan what he is going to say next as he speaks and to predict what is about to be said as he listens.

filler   The word or words used by the student to fill a gap in cloze (*qv*) or completion tests. In cloze tests the filler is usually one word only.

form   A version of a test which is in parallel with other forms, all in the same *format* but with

	different content, usually prepared for security purposes (see page 21).
format	The way in which the test material is organised, such as multiple-choice or interview.
guessing	The formula for applying a correction for guessing in a multiple-choice test is to reduce the score for each student by subtracting from the number he got right the number he got wrong divided by one less than the number of options. For example, in a three-option test, number right minus $\frac{1}{2}$ number wrong; or in a four-option test, number right minus $\frac{1}{3}$ number wrong.
item	That part of an objective test which sets the problem to be answered by the student: usually either in *multiple-choice* form as a statement (*stem*) followed by several choices (*options*) of which one is the right answer (*key*) and the rest are not (*distractors*) (see page 79); or in *true/false* form as a single statement which the student must judge to be either right or wrong (see page 28).
key	See *item*.
multiple-choice	See *item*.
normal curve	A symmetrical distribution of measurements such as that produced by large numbers of random events, idealised into a standard which is referred to for many statistical purposes (see page 14).
objective test	A test in which there is only one right answer to each *item*, so that the marking is mechanical, though considerable subjective judgement will have been used in writing the items and deciding which should be included in the test (see page 110).

options	See *item*.
rank order	The result of placing things in order of merit, from best to worst, without necessarily giving a numerical value to each of them (see page 112).
reliability	Consistency, the extent to which the scores resulting from a test are similar wherever and whenever it is taken, and whoever marks it (see page 10).
rubric	Information for the student on how to do the test, including instructions, examples, and the organisation of test procedures (see page 20).
scripted speech	Language read aloud from written text, as opposed to *unscripted speech*, which is spontaneous (see page 31).
skewed distribution	A pattern of scores in which there are more scores near the top than near the bottom (negative skew), or more scores near the bottom than near the top (positive skew) (see page 14).
specification	A description of a test (or a series of tests) which states as exactly as possible what is required for it to fulfil its purpose. The specification is usually written in advance but may well be modified by experience with the tests in practice.
stem	See *item*.
stimulus	Material used to give the student something to understand (receptive) or something to talk or write about (productive). It may be a text to be heard or read; pictures or other visuals; realia or other objects; and so on.

text	A stretch of language, either written or spoken, which is used as the basis for a test.
true/false	See *item*.
unscripted speech	Language spoken spontaneously, with false starts, repetitions, connectives (eg 'you know') and hesitation phenomena ('er', 'mm') as opposed to scripted speech, which is read aloud from a written text (see page 31).
validity	The extent to which a test measures what it is intended to measure (see page 11).

Index